THE LORD OF THE RINGS™

The Art of
THE TWO TOWERS

THE LORD OF THE RINGS™

The Art of
THE TWO TOWERS

Gary Russell

HOUGHTON MIFFLIN COMPANY
Boston · New York
2003

Library of Congress Cataloging-in-Publication Data is available.
ISBN 0-618-33130-1

Printed and bound in Belgium by Proost NV, Turnhout
HC 10 9 8 7 6 5 4 3 2 1

Editor: Chris Smith
Designer: Paul Vyse
Layout: Terence Caven
Production: Arjen Jansen

Page 1: Treebeard birthday card, pencil sketch by Alan Lee; pages 2–3:
Helm's Deep, color study by Paul Lasaine; page 6: Eye of Sauron, water-
colour by Alan Lee; page 7: Isengard, color study by Paul Lasaine; page 8:
The Golden Hall, color study by Jeremy Bennett; pages 9–13: Edoras ban-
ner designs by Gareth Jensen; page 187: Gollum, pencil sketch by John
Howe; page 188: Eye of Sauron, environment study by Jeremy Bennett;
pages 190–191: Mount Doom, matte painting by Max Dennison; page 192:
Minas Morgul, watercolor by John Howe.

Contents

Foreword

The foreword to the first volume in this series, *The Art of The Fellowship of the Ring*, ended with a promise that the paintings, sketches and designs for *The Two Towers* were going to be fantastic. Having seen a number of them while researching that first book, I was confident in that statement. But earlier this year I returned to Wellington in New Zealand to research the rest of the material, and frankly "fantastic" just could not do justice to what I saw. During the months between my visits, the bar of Peter Jackson's expectations had been raised considerably – and the quality of new artwork had improved to meet the challenge of making *The Two Towers* even more of a visual feast than *The Fellowship of the Ring*. My challenge of selecting the very best of the art for this book therefore became even more daunting – it really is a terrible task looking at all the work that the artists have put into their jobs and having to select, on average, just one in four pieces to represent both the artist and the location/creature/prop/costume that was drawn or painted or created with a computer. But with the generous help of all the artists featured here we managed to whittle the thousands of pieces down to five hundred.

A few brief grateful thanks need to be given out at this point, so please, bear with me. Thanks to Benjamin Cook and Gareth Wigmore for their sterling efforts helping me get this written up and delivered. Thanks to the marvelous Melissa Booth, who guided me around Wellington and ensured I got access to what I needed when I needed it. To Jacq and Hannah at Weta, who put up with me shambling around the Workshop and pinned artists down for me. And to Richard Taylor, who let me hold one of his well-deserved Oscar statuettes. Now, that's not something you do every day!

If the first film was packed with action and fabulous creatures, this film is richer in character and spectacle – the epic battle of Helm's Deep, the breathtaking fall of Orthanc, Frodo and Sam's journey toward Mordor and, most important, the proper introduction of one of the most famous characters in literature, Gollum. Indeed, so many new and important characters are brought into the plot in this film that there's barely room to feature them all in here.

I imagine that by now you've seen the finished film, sat back and felt pleased that for the second time in just twelve months director Peter Jackson and his talented teams have delivered on their promise and given us another exhilarating chapter in the story of Frodo and his quest to return the Ring to Mordor.

Which brings us to *The Return of the King*. Yes, I've seen some of the paintings. And yes, they, too, are fantastic. In fact, they're *amazing* . . .

Gary Russell
September 2002

Introduction

For the first book in this series, I turned the introductions over to the prime movers in this new celluloid interpretation of Tolkien's finest work: Effects Supervisor Richard Taylor, Production Designer Grant Major, Visual Art Director Paul Lasaine, Conceptual Artists John Howe and Alan Lee and, of course, Director Peter Jackson. This time around, it is time to concentrate on a few of the designers I met, based in and around the Weta Workshop in Wellington, who, even though in many cases their work on *The Lord of the Rings* was almost over, talked enthusiastically and affectionately about the project.

Supervising Storyboard Artist Christian Rivers told me how he came to be involved in the film:

"Well, I've worked with Richard and Peter since before Weta was a company as such. I started working for them in 1991 for *Brain Dead*. I storyboarded it with Peter, and then went on to work for Richard on the Special Effects crew. Weta was formed during the production of *Heavenly Creatures* in 1993 and I joined full-time a year later as a Conceptual Illustrator and Creature FX Technician for shows such as *Hercules* and *Xena*.

"When the *Lord of the Rings* project came round, we were still reeling from the fact that *King Kong* had been canned. I was actually one of the first people to do any artwork for the project; we started storyboarding as soon as Peter and Fran started writing. The first storyboards and creature designs were drawn in August 1997 and, on and off, I've been working on *The Lord of the Rings* ever since.

"As far as my background knowledge of the project was concerned, I'd read the books when I was fourteen, but only once, and I didn't remember them that well. However, I was an avid Dungeons and Dragons player and the sensibilities in the campaigns that I liked to play were very similar in tone to Tolkien's world — very grounded in reality. I didn't know it as well as a lot of the other designers on the film, who had read *The Lord of the Rings* and all the surrounding books.

"When I storyboard Peter's movies, I try not to read the scripts before we start. I know it sounds odd, but I like to get the story straight from Peter's shot-by-shot description of the film. It's basically him and me in a room. I have a drawing board and a stack of panels, and he sits there with the script and he describes each shot to me. When we first started no design work or casting had been done, so I was kind of making up the look of the characters and the sets as we went. Of course, they look completely different from the way they look in the film . . .

"Later on, as Alan Lee and John Howe were designing the sets, the Art Department was making little animatic models for us to use. We had little toy figures for all the characters that were in scale with the set models, and Peter would create the shots using them and a tiny camera. The camera was hooked up to a monitor and a video board for frame grabbing. Pete would frame the shot he wanted and yell, 'Okay, okay . . . grab that frame!' – and I would draw from the screen. Then Pete would reposition the toys and the camera and we'd move on to the next shot. This stage of drawings was very rough and I would pass off these chicken-scratch sketches to another artist, Andrew Calder, to clean up.

"The storyboarding process was basically the first stage of storyboarding the films, and like any part of the filmmaking process is ever evolving. We eventualy changed the storyboards into 3-D CGI to further assess how we would be able to create the films.

"I still find it hard to believe that I was involved in this project. It's incredible to think that I got to work on *The Lord of the Rings* and I didn't have to drive further than fifteen minutes from home to do it."

I next spoke to the man who has taken on Paul Lasaine's mantle for this film and the next, Jeremy Bennett. Although Paul did a few pieces for *The Two Towers* and *The Return of the King*, he concentrated mainly on *The Fellowship of the Ring*, which meant Jeremy could have a guiding hand over the following two movies.

"I had read the books a few times, and loved them, but more than anything I am a big fan of Alan Lee's work. To actually be working alongside him is humbling but it's also great fun. His wealth of emotional knowledge regarding Middle-earth is astonishing. If I have any questions, he can probably answer them. But yeah, I loved the books as well.

"My job as VFX Art Director is to take shots handed over from Peter Jackson and integrate the live action and blue-screen footage with the environments that we create for them. The geographical location, time of day, lighting and color palette are all elements that need to be taken into consideration and carefully balanced. The job is time-consuming but ultimately satisfying.

"I will piece all these things together and present them to Peter for comment. If we take the Dead Marshes, for example, I might present artwork for a group of shots and give Peter a variety of options so he has more to choose from. He might say, 'Well, I like that on that painting, but so-and-so I'd like to change.'

"I also have to take into account if there are any miniatures, decide where they will be placed in the artwork, what elements might be added to it, in so far as the atmosphere, massive elements, blue screen, figures walking on the miniature, waterfalls, woods, skies and so on.

"I imagine that it's unusual that I'm this involved in so many aspects of the production – but then I imagine a film that generates this much artwork is also unusual. It's rare – but I think all big-budget movies dealing responsibly with genres like this should do exactly the same.

"When I first started, I was totally thrown and wondered, 'How on earth are we going to do all that on film?,' but I quickly realized it was a gigantic endeavor, and with so many people pulling together, I knew it would be all right in the end. Of course, I still wonder how we're going to do half the things we do, and sometimes it feels formidable and a bit terrifying.

"Right now I'm doing pretty much what Paul was doing and so I can see now why I was brought on in the first place, given the number of meetings that I have to attend and the amount of time that I don't therefore spend at the drawing board. When Paul was around, I had the luxury of time to develop environments, like Isengard, and I could do fifty sketches for one shot – thinking about how it might look, how the miniature of it might be composed and so on. Now it's more of a balancing act, although in some respects it's easier because all the filming has been done and we're dealing with lots of footage that is more or less cut, so you know exactly what has to go in the final shot.

One of the most overlooked features of these movies is the miniatures – or bigatures, as they're known around Weta, because despite being miniatures in terms of their people-to-building scale ratios, many of them still took up a studio stage the size of a football field! Helm's Deep, Minas Tirith, Rivendell, the Isengard pits, were all built relatively small so cameras could move around appropriately and the characters could be computer-generated and inserted in.

Working on much of the miniature work is Mary Maclachlan, who explains how her department's work played such a big part in the films.

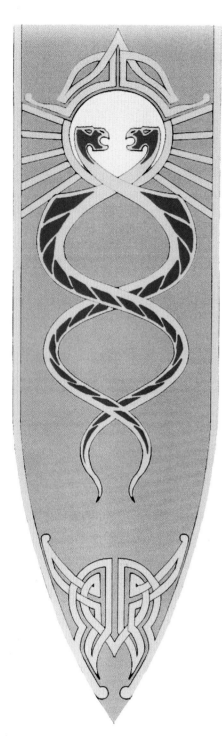

"What we do in our department is the wonderful world of model-making – making the models for *The Lord of the Rings*. That is to say we take these lovely pencil sketch drawings that Alan Lee and John Howe give us and we try to figure out how we're going to turn them into three-dimensional miniatures, as whatever size they may turn out to be is often governed by the size of the studio.

"So we take their drawings and we figure out how we're going to build them – be it a castle or a ravine or a cave or a cavern – and, in conjunction with Alan and John and Richard Taylor and Peter Jackson, we sit down and really figure out how it's going to fit in with the sets that have to be built for the actors to walk in – like, for example, Rivendell or Helm's Deep. Then Grant Major is involved, because some of the miniatures have to be drawn or drafted to match the sets that are going to be built. Some models, such as Zirak-zigil, are never going to be seen as a set – at least as far as I know, certainly not extensively – and they were built purely from the drawings. We have one beautiful view of a tower in its environment, perhaps an atmospheric pencil drawing, and they say, 'Oh well, okay, let's make it.'

"We're governed by the ceiling in the studio, which is twenty-two feet approximately, so if it's a tall tower on top of a tall rock, we think, 'Well, how much tower and how much rock do we need to see to match in with the environment?' And if they're going to be shooting some real mountains and rocks (because the drawings are often based on a location as well – lucky Alan and John got to go to all the locations, which, sadly, we didn't), we would see the photographs of some of them, and then we'd see the sketches based on those photographs. Then we see all those elements together – location photos, the storyboards, the drawings – and *then* we have input from Peter, who says what the actions are that are probably going to be taking place, or what he feels the building may have to do, especially if it's going to be destroyed or someone's going to come bursting out of a wall.

"Now, before we build a full-size model, what we do is we build maquettes. Just as they do with the creatures and the characters, we do a three-dimensional sketch in Plasticine, which is no more than perhaps a foot or a couple of feet tall, just to have a look at any issues that might arise during the construction of it. And also, if there's action to happen – if, for example, something has to be broken away or fall apart, or

things have got to be CG'd in, which is often the case – they can have a good look at it with a little pencil-cam, and say, 'Yeah, yeah, this is good,' or 'No, we need a bit more space there,' or 'We need that doorway more over there.' Often, further drawings might be made to demonstrate how to extend a part, and then we'll do another maquette or we'll alter that maquette, and then finally they'll say, 'Yeah – that's good. That's great! That works perfectly,' and then we'll build a full-sized one.

"Film miniatures – certainly for this particular film – have to be very large, because there are a lot of things that have to go on in and around them. You have to put actors into them, so you have to be able to sustain a good scale for your rock, brick, windows, doors and all that kind of stuff, and the scenery, the trees, the shrubbery that has to be put into them – they have to look realistic, so they have to be very big to stand up to that sort of scale. If you do really tiny models, when you put them on a big screen in the cinema, they're going to look like toys. Now, having said that, Barad-dûr was built as a very tall tower, but in actual fact it was only 1:66 scale – an actual scale, which is N-gauge for model railroad enthusiasts. But because it's not based on any contemporary shapes in the sense that people can't see doors and windows that they recognize, because it's more of an evil, malevolent, amorphous sort of shape, with all these spikes and towers and gantries and walkways and things going on, people don't realize the scale. You can get away with it!

"Now, Helm's Deep as a scale was at 1/35th scale, which actually is fairly small – the little figures on them would have been two inches tall. And Helm's Deep as a model was fairly big – it was probably about fifteen to twenty feet across, and it was in a huge valley that was thirty feet across, so it was really quite a big model set. That was actually the very first miniature that we built. John Baster started work on that; he had already started when I came on board so he did the bulk of the work on Helm's Deep. When I arrived, they were just roughing out the shape of it – Grant Major was involved as well, because that's one of the models that also appears as a set, so they built live-action sections of it. They also built a quarter-scale model of it – which we weren't involved in – that was more of a set than a miniature, as it was halfway between the two. They used it as a false perspective effect, so that they could have foreground armies and the fortress in the background and still have it looking pretty big.

"I only found out the other day that Zirak-zigil was back in the film. We built the miniature but heard they weren't going to use it in the end – I think they were going to do it digitally, or just talk about what happened. Zirak-zigil was drawn in pencil and ink by John Howe and he had this beautiful tower on top of an angular rock – like the Matterhorn, very precipitous with lots of snow and ice – and the idea is that inside of it there's a spiral staircase that comes up from the deep caverns beneath Moria. The Balrog and Gandalf have a grand old chase up it, and they come out at the top and have a spectacular fight. We did a maquette (see page 18), and they were very happy with it pretty much as it was done. It was probably about ten and a half feet tall, made out of Plasticine, and then we built the miniature. The miniature is actually one of the smaller miniatures, probably only about thirteen feet tall; it has a spiral staircase, the windows all show through, and there's a broken-out hole where it's been damaged before. So, it's of a reddish rock, and crumbling and worn in places – the tower has been there for millennia – but it's all covered in snow at the top, and Gandalf comes tearing out followed by the Balrog. The Balrog bursting out of the top will probably be done digitally rather than using the miniature and breaking it – but I'm not sure yet. I haven't seen the amended storyboards for that. Although we worked on this a long time ago I'm rather pleased it's now going to be used.

"We tend to be very architecturally honest. By that I mean if our miniature was built to a scale we could walk around it, and it would all look very real – we'd get to the rooms we wanted to get to. Helm's Deep and Rivendell were certainly like that, where the internal structure of rooms and corridors was all logically laid out. Also, the camber has to be correct, the cobblestones – right down to the guttering. Everything has to be correct. We even got little braziers and lanterns and they all had to be correct at the small scale at which we built them because when you see the big scenes, you're going to see it all for real.

"With windows and doors, they have to look as ornate and sculpted on the miniatures as they do on the sets. We were all working from the same beautiful drawings by Alan – he does lovely renderings, so we were able to recreate all of the architecture from looking at his drawings. They're quite beautifully done, but still allow us

a little room for interpretation, as we have to produce a three-dimensional object from a flat drawing. So we logically follow through the architecture ourselves and make it look quite plausible.

"Sometimes we would do things like the wall panels and the brick parapets as a section, a flat piece of artwork with all the buttresses on. We would then mold them off, and then repeat them all around, so we would only have to do the one section – then cut and paste it. But when you look at things like the citadel at Minas Tirith you have some fine architecture in there – that's done very specifically and carefully, as are the roofs and the roof patterns, but we can still make a roof pattern mold. At 1/35th scale, you have to be able to see a little bit of depth and texture so that this shows up on the camera and under the lighting. And, of course, every single building has a different texture because it's from a different part of the world. This was a challenge but not impossible. After all, there's no such thing as an unsolvable problem. That's what the challenge of model-making is. The art of it, if you like, is producing all these buildings and textures and effects to bring those pictures to life."

One of the key people in helping bring those pictures to life was Digital Matte Artist Roger Kupelian. He explained to me what his role was and how it fit into the scheme of things:

"A Digital Matte Artist is a painter first, digital artist second, and quite often that is the approach one had to take when producing matte shots for the films. The world of *The Lord of the Rings* that is being incorporated into the film is based on original art by illustrators such as Alan Lee, so it springs from a very subjective frame of mind. Regardless of the wonderful vistas that New Zealand provides, and the photographic reference sometimes offered, sometimes thrust into the development of the image, the matte painting is a painting in a very real sense: it has to convey a story. This story begins with a sketch by Alan Lee or a quick paint sketch by Jeremy Bennett. Sometimes Gus Hunter will give us a bit more in terms of a Photoshop layout. Once we get the green light (quite often Peter approves the 'feel' of a shot more than anything else), we begin painting, first roughly, to lay the image out accurately and match it to the live plate, then more definitely. Since changing a painting in its later history is not as simple as changing lighting on a shader and rerendering, great care is often

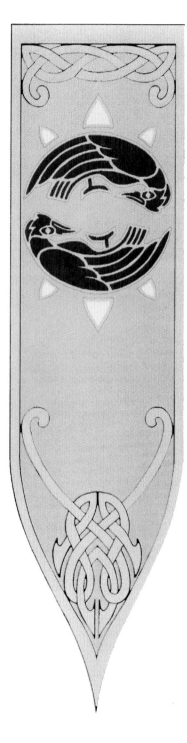

taken in making sure that each step is successful. Sometimes we'll even film a rougher painting to see how much more is actually needed. For others, such as the painting on page 133, we might overpaint, put in more than will ever be seen, just in case.

"Of course, there are paintings that were fairly simple sky replacements, where the matte painter acted like a digital compositor, in a sense using digital tools to replace one image with another without working too hard, but those instances were quite rare. Photos rarely do the trick in and of themselves. The difference between a digital compositor and a matte artist is that they usually have many other concerns (in the case of *The Lord of the Rings*, quite weighty, technical ones) and a variety of tasks to tackle. Our two worlds have a gray area between them, but there is quite a distinction in terms of focus: a simple way to put it would be, one is a photographer on wheels, and the other is a painter, but both can be animators."

My next port of call was to talk to three of the most prolific designers represented in this volume – Daniel Falconer, Ben Wootten and Warren Mahy. Daniel first:

"I was employed here at the end of 1996 as a designer on *King Kong*, which consequently fell through – early in the following year – but I stayed on as a designer and a general workshop guy. And then, when *The Lord of the Rings* reared its head in 1997, I was one of a bunch of about five or six guys who began working on that.

"I think it helped that I am a huge fan of the books. It meant I was already very familiar with the material – to the point that, throughout the production, I'd often get calls from people whom I'd never met saying, 'We need this question answered very quickly and we've heard that you're the person who either can answer it or knows where to go and find this information in the books!' I've also read *The Silmarillion* and a lot of the other material, so it was fantastic to be able to use information like that in the workplace.

"As a reader of the books, I had a visual idea of what everything looked like to me, but I think my ideas were – what's the word? – diffused enough not to exclude other ideas and other suggestions. I mean, a lot of the time, I found my thoughts weren't entirely dissimilar to what Peter was asking for. Generally, when he asked for something, if he hadn't given us an explicit brief, obviously the first thing I did was think, 'I've always imagined it to look like

such-and-such' and then we'd go from there. Often, he had quite specific ideas about what he wanted to see, and I would obviously try to deliver what he asked for but also give him options, give him ideas that were maybe more like what I was thinking – and I can't think offhand of any times when they jarred enormously. Which was lucky, I guess.

"What often happens in a workshop like this is that we have a system – particularly with creatures such as the Watcher in the Water, and the Uruk-hai armor – whereby we would give Pete some options to begin with and he'd say, 'Okay, yeah, these are kind of nice, but let's throw away all preconceptions here. Let's open up extremely wide. Let's just go for it – from one end of the spectrum to the other.' And often he'd push us down that path for a while first, right to some very extreme versions. I mean, there were some ideas for the Watcher in the Water that were big seal-like creatures. There were others that were arthropods . . . And once we'd gone to the absolute limits of imagination, then he'd pull us back and we'd focus on something – often that was not entirely dissimilar to some of the very earliest ideas. But it's in that exploration that you'll find lots of neat little features that will then be used in the final concept. That's probably why – on the Watcher in the Water, for example, or the Uruk-hai armor – there was quite a range of different ideas drawn up before we nailed it.

"There's loads of cross-pollination here. We were all in one big room together, so everybody could feed off each other. You can wander around and see what everybody else is doing if you're feeling a bit dry – and it'll immediately spin off ideas in you! And we'd all talk about it while we were working. Everybody brings their elements to it. And what you end up with is so much richer than any one person could ever have conceived of – that's really satisfying, to know you've been part of that team – but there's enough of it there onscreen that you go, 'Wow, that's my creature, but it's been brought to life!'

"It was helpful, too, to put on music that was suitable to what we were designing at the time. Peter always kept coming back to the movie *Braveheart* as having the closest look to that which he wanted in terms of realism, so the *Braveheart* soundtrack was, logically, something that we worked to quite a lot. Likewise, *Last of the Mohicans* had the feeling that we wanted, so we often listened to that as well. When we were designing the Uruk-hai, we used to listen to a lot of a band called Tool, because the angrier, heavy stuff really suited it and got us in the right mood. In fact, the band is visiting, coming to see what they've inspired!

"So I've been working on this film for five or six years now and it has been phenomenally thrilling for me to be able to see designs that we did, nearly five years ago in some cases, appearing on the screen. That is very, very rewarding."

And now over to Ben Wootten:

"I joined when we were working on *King Kong,* so I've been here, wow, six years. I started the same time as Daniel and Shaun Bolton. About three or four months after Jamie Beswarick, I think.

"It's crazy, because I'm a huge fan of the books and couldn't believe we were doing the movie. I went to university in Dunedin and I had friends down there that were great fans of the books as well. And I remember many late-night talks about what you would do if you were going to make it into a film – who you'd cast, and things like that. And to suddenly find myself, eight years later, designing on the films . . . It's totally surreal.

"Working with John Howe was amazing. I've had his artwork on my walls for ages. And to work with him was fantastic. To work from his sketches for the Balrog was probably the most amazing thing. Insane, too. It's very hard not to actually put something on a pedestal above other stuff.

"Sadly for me, it's basically over – I'm on to other things here at Weta. For most of us on the design team, that's the case. Sometimes there's some callback to Digital about creature design or things like that – for upcoming creatures. I know Warren is still going over there for the Wargs and other things, but apart from the merchandising we've done – all the statues, plaques and figures, which is kind of exciting – it means that, short of maybe going over and seeing the latest stuff that's being worked on at Weta Digital every now and then, the film's finished for us.

"Of course, by the time we get to see the second two, it'll all be pretty fresh again. We'll have forgotten or may not have known how things actually ended up.

"One of the things that I think makes the design more successful is the fact that we all work together, swapping ideas and information around. No one works in a vacuum. I think that's important – it makes our job not just

easier, it makes it far more realistic and far more successful. And far more fun!"

Finally, let's turn our attention to Warren Mahy:

"I went to school with Ben Wootten, right from primary school, intermediate and all the rest of it. Then he went away to university, and I didn't see him for ten years, but one day he contacted me and said that there was a project that was happening that I should be involved with. Other than doing stuff at school with Ben, I never trained, didn't go to art school, and in fact I'd ended up being a printer. He said that he thought it was still worth me sending down any work that I had to Richard Taylor here at Weta. And I did, and it basically happened from there. Richard got me down on the strength of the work that I'd done, and I was brought into the design team. I hadn't read the books for maybe ten years or so – I read them at school, and Ben and I had a big group of friends that were into role-playing, so we knew the books pretty well, but as soon as I knew what the project was I read them again.

"The great thing about the team here was that if there wasn't any design work to do, you could do other stuff – Richard would get you fiberglassing, or carving poly, or going out molding trees or picking leaves, or something. I've basically had a paid apprenticeship in the last five years – in filmmaking!

"The fantastic thing about being involved in *The Lord of the Rings* is that so many people say, 'There has been no film like this taking up this length of time. Nothing comparable where you can spend so much time delving into different characters and spending the time getting it to its nth degree.' And part of that for me was actually having the time to learn all the different processes rather than jumping into a six-month project, and within three months all the design work has to be done and inevitably you don't get to be able to produce your best work, because you do it so quickly.

"Because I was quite happy to spend time on set as well, just as a set dresser, I spent some time on one of the mountains where they were filming. So if Richard wanted anything designed there he could grab me; in this way I ended up designing Sauron's sword on top of a mountain, on the back of somebody's call sheet. I remember I was just sitting in the snow, and looking down at Richard and Peter Jackson, who had just starting filming, and thinking, 'This is cool! This is a good job!' "

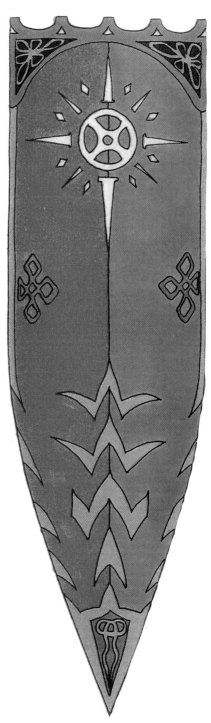

◁◁ **ZIRAK-ZIGIL**
Color study
Jeremy Bennett
A study of the peak of Zirak-zigil environment.

ZIRAK-ZIGIL
Color studies
Jeremy Bennett
"These are environment studies for where Gandalf and the
Balrog emerge, still fighting, on what might as well be the
roof of the world. I was thinking about the area and how it
might look. They are color keys — I tried to make each one
different to give Peter a range of possibilities. These are
pretty old, done at a stage when we were unsure as to how
far this whole sequence was going to go in terms of being
filmed, so I decided to create the same elements but in
different compositions."

ZIRAK-ZIGIL ◇
Color studies
Jeremy Bennett
"Here are four frames of quite an elaborate set of storyboards. A number of us had three or
four attempts at working on this, presenting ideas to Peter. This was one idea that I took a bit
further. You can follow the fight, then the Balrog dropping and then finally all this eventually
leads to the transformation of Gandalf. It's actually a total metamorphosis for him."

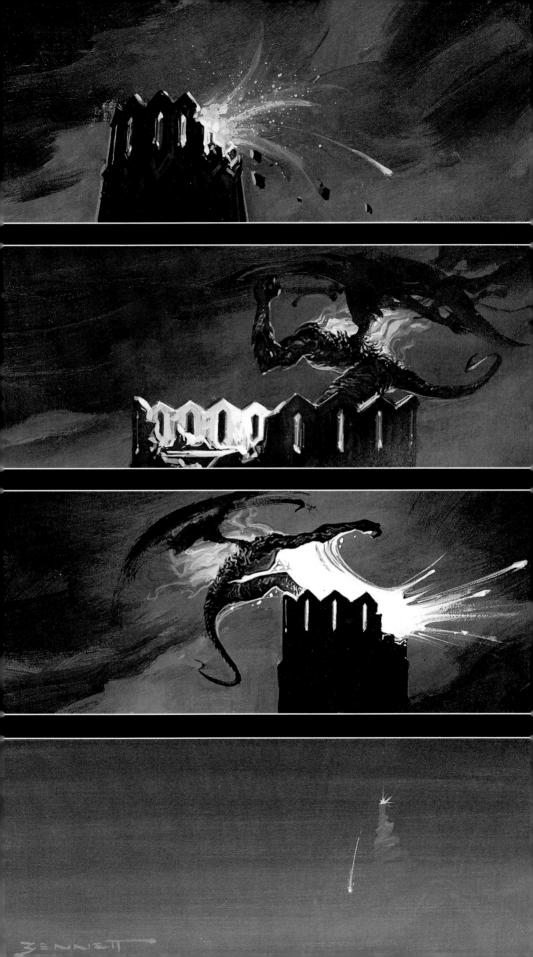

ZIRAK-ZIGIL
Pencil sketches
John Howe

"Zirak-zigil is one of the Mountains of Moria, upon which the Dwarves built an observation tower, the culmination of the Endless Stair. It had to feel precarious and lofty: imagine going up all those steps only to emerge on some pleasant flat terrace. The top is weathered and broken to allow Gandalf and the Balrog to emerge — I couldn't imagine the Dwarves actually sunning themselves at the top on pleasant days, but more peering through slit windows at the world below."

KHAZAD-DÛM
Pencil sketch and digital artwork
Alan Lee
"There's an amazing sequence at the beginning of <u>The Two Towers</u> where we follow Gandalf and the Balrog down the chasm and we have a wide shot showing the 'Roots of the Mountains' and the lake that they splash down into. I also did drawings for the Endless Stair and the nameless creatures that might have watched their progress. The drawing on the left was the original idea, which was further developed in the study above."

THE BALROG
Pencil sketch
Sourisak Chanpaseuth
"I was given the task of drawing a slime Balrog. Although it's so obviously broken down, deteriorating into something different, and its wings are burned away, it is clearly similar to its former self."

THE BALROG
Pencil sketch
Johnny Brough
Johnny offered up an alternative for the slime Balrog, showing a far more skeletal version, as if the pool has stripped him of everything that makes him what he is, and yet never diminishing the malevolence he projects.

THE BALROG
Pencil sketch
John Howe
"The sequence where Gandalf falls with the Balrog is one of my absolute favorites in the story. The Balrog turns into a 'creature of slime' before crawling back up the Endless Stair to reignite on Zirak-zigil. Once his fire is extinguished, I imagined him as skeletal, diminished."

THE BALROG
Color sketch
Daniel Falconer
"Trying to imagine how the Balrog might accomplish his transformation from a fiery demon to a thing of slime, I imagined his skin hardening like a crust on lava. Meanwhile, internally he liquefies, exuding a thick black oil from between the cracks of his cooled skin."

THE BALROG
Color sketch
Christian Rivers
"This Balrog was actually drawn before any of the other ones. It was to show him coming out of the water, and that he's just erupting in steam and then cooling, like lava or molten metal going into water. You can see fire creeping out, and there's a little bit of fire spitting like blood out from his mouth and stuff — I wanted to show him really feeling pain."

THE BALROG
Color sketches
Christian Rivers

"The drawing on the left was just a concept, really — kind of a different approach to what everyone else was offering Peter. I was a little worried about the Slime Balrog, as a lot of the designs had started taking it in a direction that had it mutating and changing form. I approached him as how a physical creature would look if it were made of lava and was dipped in water. As it struggled its skin would crack and tear as the water tried to cool it — parts of its 'flesh' would be eaten away and hardened. What you are left with is this weird, almost scarred, muscular rock.

"The image below shows the same concept but as it could appear happening on screen. It shows the lava spitting off and reacting with the water, becoming pressurized and exploding outward as the Balrog twists in agony, engulfed by a cloud of steam. A really violent collision of the elements."

THE BALROG
Color sketch
Christian Rivers

"Gandalf's battle with the Balrog at the start of the film picks up from the initial drop down Khazad-dûm into this lake. Then the Balrog comes out all slimy and dripping and falling to bits. So, basically, I imagined a progression. He falls into the lake and his fire's extinguished, but there's still this deep hot core of him on fire. And then he emerges and he starts changing from having slimy bits dripping off him, which isn't slime — I saw it more as lava cooling through the cracks in his skin. This picture shows where the lava and the water have cooled — a bit like if you drop molten lead into water it forms all of these kinds of hard shapes. So this is him, as he's cooling and he's starting to crack and then he eventually erupts . . ."

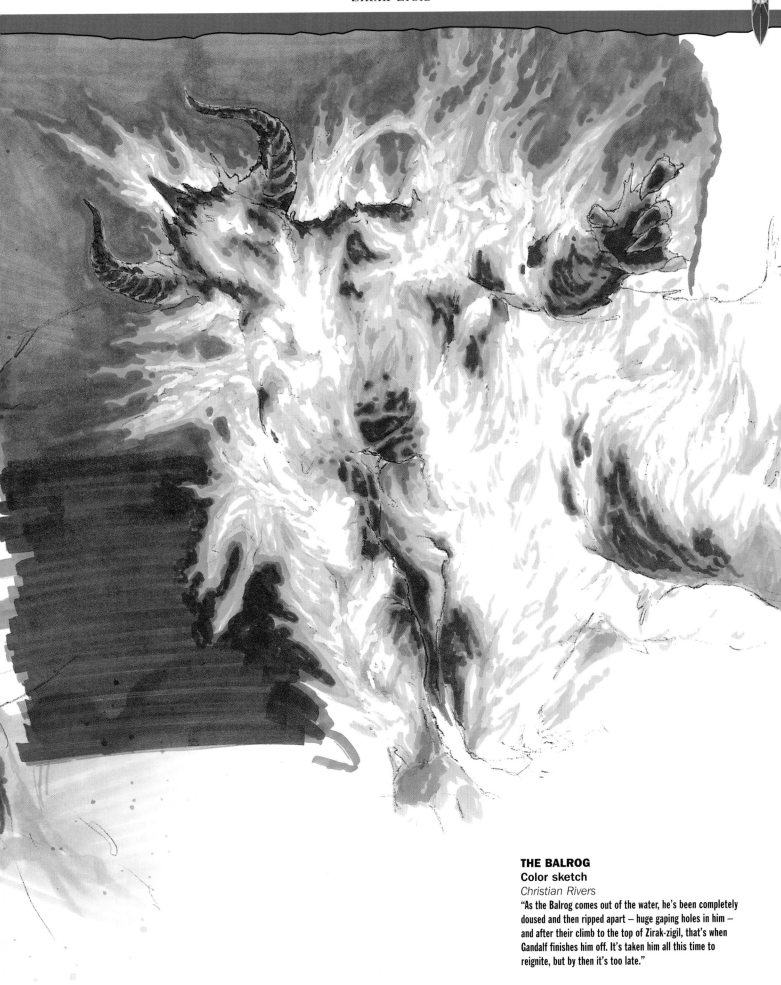

THE BALROG
Color sketch
Christian Rivers
"As the Balrog comes out of the water, he's been completely doused and then ripped apart — huge gaping holes in him — and after their climb to the top of Zirak-zigil, that's when Gandalf finishes him off. It's taken him all this time to reignite, but by then it's too late."

EMYN MUIL

EMYN MUIL
Studies

Alan Lee & Yanick Dusseault
The Emyn Muil is the rocky wilderness that Frodo and Sam cross, stalked by Gollum. Above is Yanick's study for his final matte painting (seen on previous spread). The other images are sketches for various shots in the sequence by Alan.

EMYN MUIL
Digital composites
Yanick Dusseault
The images on these pages are a further
selection of matte paintings by Yanick, which
have been seamlessly composited into the
studio and location shots.

FANGORN

LASAINE

FANGORN
Lighting studies
Paul Lasaine

Top: "This is the finished Fangorn painting — one of my favorites. There's also a digital version of this [see previous spread] where I took the design even further for Grant Major — with more trees. In the middle is the first Fangorn image I painted. I wanted it to look really creepy, almost like an old graveyard. At the bottom is an early painting of where Merry and Pippin find themselves lost in the forest."

▽ **FANGORN**
Color studies
Paul Lasaine
"These 'Fangorn with Merry and Pippin' paintings were done to show how Fangorn could look creepy as well as beautiful and lush simply by changing the color of the light."

 FANGORN
Color studies
Paul Lasaine
Paul painted these ideas for the sequence in which Aragorn, Legolas and Gimli enter the forest and encounter the reborn Gandalf the White. Paul wanted the light to bleed out of the figure of Gandalf and slowly illuminate the whole forest.

GANDALF THE WHITE
Costume design sketch
Ngila Dickson
"To contrast Gandalf the White with his previous Grey incarnation, I used fewer layers and much lighter and more delicate fabrics for his robes and quilted tunic. Also, the lines are much cleaner and more defined to signify that he has just been newly minted."

FANGORN ◊
Digital artwork
Alan Lee
"The image to the right involved taking a live action plate which was shrunk down and then the edge of Fangorn was extended, as were the Rohan Plains."

FANGORN
Pencil sketches
Alan Lee

Two ideas (left, and opposite bottom) for the look of the trees. "We looked at a number of possible locations for these shots of the interior of the forest, but Brian Massey and the Greens Department managed to create some memorable studio sets which more than answered our needs."

FANGORN
Color study
Alan Lee
For this design for Wellinghall, I made the set even bigger by framing it with a shot of the Fangorn miniature.

FANGORN
Pen drawing
Alan Lee
A study of the Fangorn environment for those constructing the miniature forest.

TREEBEARD
Color scheme
Christian Rivers
"An early conceptual work – drawn in '97 – that focuses on Treebeard's deep glowing eyes. Tolkien described them as 'like looking into a deep pool' but I made them look too magical and completely wrong, as Treebeard is a likable character. Yet here he's an absolute nightmare!"

ENT
Pencil sketch
Sacha Lees
"The sketch opposite shows the scale between an Ent and a hobbit. I like the tree-root on this – my concept for the Ents was that they're extremely treelike and yet all the different parts, like the roots and the branches, form limbs."

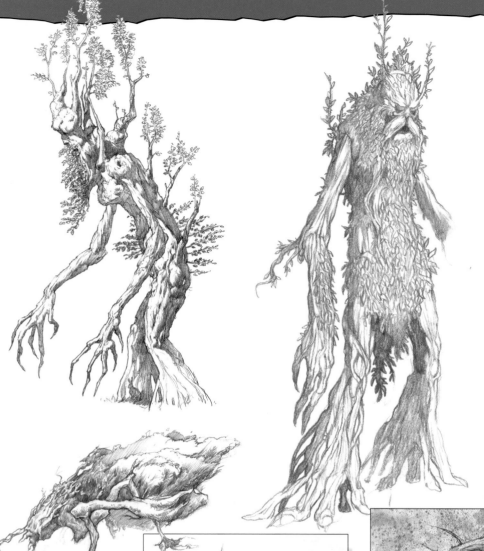

◊ **ENTS**
Pencil sketches
Christian Rivers
"With the drawing far left, I was trying to lose much of the humanoid feel by doubling them right over, so they're still woodlike creatures that are part tree but not necessarily completely man-shaped. I wanted to get away from the idea of a man that's made out of wood and break the silhouette in any way possible. I was trying to alter the proportions by giving him a long torso, long thin arms and thick stocky legs — trying to use the construction of a tree.

"The one near left is the first Ent that I drew. The Ents really are the hardest of Tolkien's creations to realize. In text it's fine, but actually showing this on film is tough. Maybe we could have seen the Ents played more like 15-foot-tall giants that have an unnatural lifespan. Treebeard would be an old man, bent over, who would stand in one spot for two years and grow moss on his skin, which would be leathery like bark, and it would be all dusty and have saplings growing out of it where the earth and the moss had gathered around his shoulder. He would be something that connects — something organic that has grown into the ground rather than grown from the ground."

ENTS ◊
Pencil sketches
Warren Mahy
"I think I was drawing sketches of the Warg at the time so I didn't have a lot to do with the Ents, mainly because Dan had got it so right from the beginning. The one to the right is a very slim-looking Ent.

"The drawing above it is something that was quite different from the normal Ent concept. This was one who wouldn't have to stand up but just developed in this way — more like a bush growing in the wind."

◊ ENT
Color sketch
Sacha Lees
"With this Ent I imagined it was like a contortionist tree, so that when you first look at it, it's a tree, and then it folds out of itself and unravels into these limbs, but not limbs like a human at all. It starts to have a life of its own as soon as it starts to move."

ENT
Pencil sketch
Daniel Falconer
"I did a couple of drawings of quite large Ents. I figured there would be Ents of varying sizes and shapes and I liked the idea that there are a couple of big heavy guys – these are the guys that would tear at the walls of Isengard. Ultimately, it wasn't an idea that was picked up, but I just loved the visual image that here's Treebeard and his old Ents who are the elders, and then coming striding through them twice as tall are these big, powerful, deep-forest Ents that would come in and actually do the heavy work."

ENTS ◊
Color sketches
Daniel Falconer

"I tried to design an Ent that didn't have a beard. The books were ambiguous on this, which left me wondering, 'Well, is Treebeard the only one with a beard, or is his just the most pronounced and unusual looking?' Ultimately, Peter did like the idea that all the Ents would have a beard of some sort, so in this case, instead of a beard, he almost has a goatee.

"One of the things I was aware of was that wherever we were going to film these, unless we built a complete set in a studio, we were probably going to end up filming them in a New Zealand forest. It would make no sense to design trees based on exotic woods, as we'd then have to put them in a New Zealand forest and they'd look out of place. The actual location for Fangorn wasn't decided upon for a long time — until well after we'd designed a lot of Ents — and it was eventually agreed that a lot of it would be studio-based. That actually opened us up to going a bit wider with our designs."

◊ **TREEBEARD**
Pencil sketch
Daniel Falconer

"This was the first Ent drawing done. Pete had said that he was very worried that the Ents would be potentially very difficult to do on film, but he really warmed to this drawing, saying, 'That's actually quite a good look, so maybe we can actually do this and do it well.' And while Treebeard did change a bit, Pete kept coming back to this first drawing and saying, 'Well, that's really the point I want to start from.'"

◊ **ENT**
Color sketch
Daniel Falconer

"This one has a very caricatured military look. He's quite a short Ent. I gave him very short stubby legs — I liked the idea that perhaps he'd wobble around. He has a lot of vegetation, so perhaps he's a younger Ent."

TREEBEARD
Color sketch
Daniel Falconer

"By this stage, we had really started to lock down what Treebeard would look like, and I thought I'd start playing with the color schemes. His beard is very heavily mossed, quite green. I also liked the idea of his bark being old and gray and gnarled, so that's what we have here.

"He's towering over the hobbits — I think there's a piece in the book where he looks at them: 'Aah, little Orcs' — thinking that they're actually Orcs, but they say, 'No, no, we're hobbits! Don't squash us!'

"And there's an interesting idea with the hands, which seem really quite out of proportion, but they're not. It's a perspective thing in this drawing. It wasn't totally successful, but I wanted to give the idea that his head was actually a lot higher up and further away from where his hands and feet were."

TREEBEARD
Digital artwork
Alan Lee
"Pippin takes a tumble."

TREEBEARD
Pencil sketches

Daniel Falconer

"I really like the idea that the hobbits are right next to Treebeard and yet have no idea he's there – they just think he's a tree but he's quietly watching them.

"By putting the hobbits in, it gave Pete an idea of scale. If anything, I think the one where they're on the outcrop is probably not far off the correct scale."

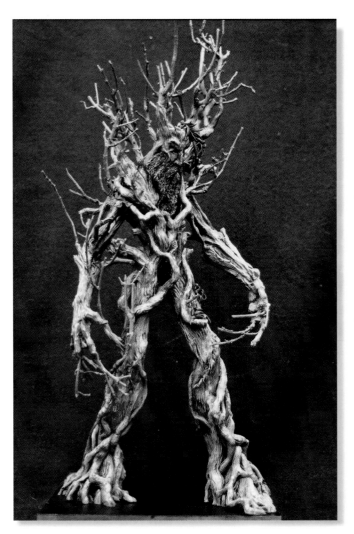

ENTS
Maquettes
Daniel Falconer
"We experimented with different Ent body proportions, trying to break out of human form by extending or shrinking their arms and legs. We also explored the balance between how much man and how much tree would comprise their final forms. Some were more man-like (top left) but Treebeard (top right) was closer to a tree. Peter approved this foot-and-a-half maquette and it became the bible reference for Treebeard."

TREEBEARD
Digital artwork
Alan Lee
"Grishnákh's first view of Treebeard."

ENTS
Digital artwork
Alan Lee

"We decided that there would be a total of nine different Ents, with variations on those to make up the numbers on the busier shots. As the final designs were being digitally modeled, they were sent back to the VFX Art Department for further development on their characters, their textures and their beards and foliage.

   "At the bottom right is one of a number of studies of Treebeard's eyes, and opposite is another of Daniel's maquettes."

Verts:	1500	0	0
Edges:	2910	0	0
Faces:	1112	0	0
UVs:	1605	0	0

THE DEAD MARSHES

THE DEAD MARSHES
Color studies
Jeremy Bennett

"These were done to give some thought to the overall color palette for the marshes. I prefer the small one on the far right, but Pete's gone for the big one — something a little brighter just to bring up the greens, so it looks a little more spooky. It probably ties in well with the spectral corpses when you see them. The idea here was to think about how much visibility you'd get around the marshes. Originally they were more claustrophobic, but Peter wanted to see four or five kilometers out into the distance so you'd really get this feeling for how large an expanse the environment was — and how easily you could become lost in there."

SPECTRAL CORPSES
Pencil sketch
Warren Mahy

"This was right at the beginning – the very first day. Richard Taylor came over to me and said, 'I need a picture of corpses. Just come up with what you can.' The idea that we were going with at that stage was that these were animated dead bodies ranging from rotting corpses to those just recently killed.

"So Frodo falls into the water, sinks down and as he's pushing the reeds aside, these corpses appear through the reflections of the water, swimming toward him."

SPECTRAL CORPSES
Pencil sketch
Sourisak Chanpaseuth

"This one is meant to be really bloated, as though it's been soaking in water – soaking throughout the First and Second Ages. I based his costume on the Rohan soldiers. I know the Rohirrim weren't meant to be there, but I think this picture tries to captures the warrior, the tragedy of the spectral corpse."

SPECTRAL CORPSES
Pencil sketch
Warren Mahy

"Frodo is way down in the reeds, and he's trying to fight his way out, but he's been surrounded by these shapes. I can imagine that the eddies in the water would change the shapes quite often. Potentially at one moment it could be a Gondorian spectral image in front of him, and then it's an Orc, and so on. Actually, that's not true, because Pete had talked a lot about the fact that he didn't want Orcs in there — he didn't want to confuse people into thinking that the Orcs were chasing him under the water. So we just concentrated on Elven and Gondorian-type characters."

SPECTRAL CORPSES
Pencil sketches
Warren Mahy

"Two sketches that give an idea of the corpses' facial expressions and what it would be like seeing the faces close up. The one near left is viewed looking down into the water from the top. Both show how the light would be reflected in the eyes, and the distance to the surface of the water."

◊ THE DEAD MARSHES
Digital artwork
Gus Hunter

"The images on the left were produced to answer Peter's brief for a more ethereal look to the corpses that Frodo sees once he's underwater. The main image on pages 48 and 49 combines live action elements which were altered on the computer to create an eerie atmosphere."

THE DEAD MARSHES
Digital artwork
Alan Lee

"These two images were to show a less spectral, more corporeal look."

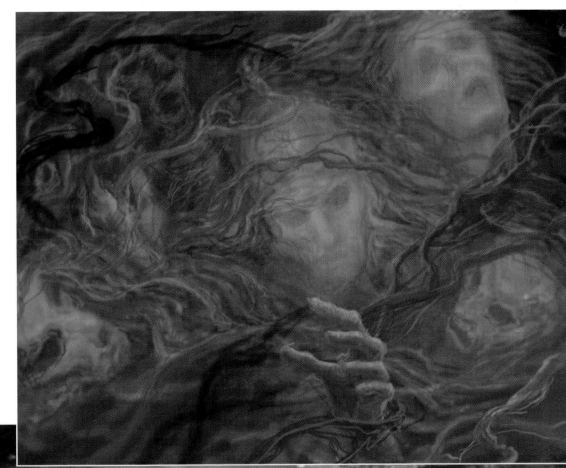

THE DEAD MARSHES
Color studies

Jeremy Bennett

"These were very simple shots to do, just general imagery
for the marshes. The large one is a color study exploring
the misted-out quality of the environment. The smaller
one was the last frame from the helicopter flyover when
they filmed out on location. In the background of the shot
as it appears in the film, we'll see Mordor way off in the
distance."

THE DEAD MARSHES
Color studies
Gus Hunter
The color panels on the left were created by Gus on the
computer to offer different looks for the lights that play
over the surface of the water.

THE DEAD MARSHES
Color study
Jeremy Bennett
"This is a small color study
exploring the relationship between
the Dead Marshes and Mordor off
in the distance."

257.3_2-1 24mm RM 107

THE DEAD MARSHES
Digital artwork
Gus Hunter
Elijah Wood had been filmed suspended above a wind machine, and shot in slow motion to create the right look for Frodo underwater. The top image by Gus has some of the other filmed material added as a guide for the compositors, while Alan's study to the left is an earlier version.

EDORAS

◁◁ EDORAS
Color study
Jeremy Bennett
A sky study for the Edoras environment.

THÉODEN
Costume design sketches
Ngila Dickson

"When we first meet Théoden, we see him as a crumpled old man, incapable of any kind of decision-making. I wanted him to have the appearance of someone who never got out of his bathrobe! So we made him three layers of gowns, all of which were bled of their color — so that deep browns became musty and rich golds a sickly yellow, while the elaborate embroidery was aged down until only the subtlest hint of the original opulence remained. On top of everything, we heaped a vast coat with a ratty-looking fur collar."

Once Gandalf has freed him from Saruman's spell, the reborn Théoden appears in a shorter, more active style of tunic and cape made in colorful, richly embroidered fabrics more fitting for the warrior king he has now become.

THÉODEN'S ARMOR
Color sketches
Daniel Falconer

"Théoden is the king, so if any member of the Rohirrim is going to have an elaborate helmet, it should be him; therefore Théoden's helmet comprises three or four different metals. It's also covered in ornate filigree. I looked a lot at the material that was pulled out of the Sutton Hoo burial mound for inspiration. There are little enamel panels, the horse's head, sun emblems, and a Celtic curl that we used time and time again.

"The earliest of the Théoden drawings here is the bottom right one – too generic, I think. It wasn't really specific enough – there wasn't anything that said Rohan culture. What we see in the lower left drawing is very close to the final armor that was made. Interestingly, on his lames, as they crisscross his stomach, there's actually a tiny hunting scene etched onto them. We thought that his armor would tell a story, so if you're ever able to see it up close, there are little soldiers chasing a boar and hunting other animals.

"The horse motif pops up again and again, so we adopted that and also put the golden sun, which is the flag of Rohan, on the shields. It was very helpful to develop these iconic devices that we would use again, so that when you see a character in Rohan armor, it doesn't matter whereabouts from Rohan he comes from – an audience member, without even questioning himself, would think, 'Oh, he's from Rohan,' as opposed to 'Who's that guy? Where's he from?' There are many peoples and cultures in <u>The Lord of the Rings</u>, so it was really important that we had these strong visual styles and color palettes to distinguish each culture and make it easier for the audience to recognize what they're looking at."

GRÍMA WORMTONGUE
Costume design sketch
Ngila Dickson

"I wanted Gríma to have the look of a hunched, feral creature who was clothed in finery but who never washed. His linen shirt was greasy, dirty and utterly repulsive – I'm happy to say it was a near perfect example of costume breakdown! The sleeves of his under-robe came to points on the hands, heightening the sense of evil intent, while the over-robe – black velvet flecked with gold – had a fishtail extension that dragged along the floor behind him. With the addition of a high, ruched-velvet collar, his neck seemed to disappear into his shoulders, creating the illusion of humped-back deformity."

GRÍMA WORMTONGUE
Color sketch
Daniel Falconer

"Wormtongue's dagger was designed to look as cold and lethal as possible. Its blade is slightly tongued as a play on his name."

ÉOWYN
Costume design sketches
Ngila Dickson

"For the character of Éowyn, I started with Tolkien's description of her as 'fair and cold.' This resulted in the simple white gown which she is wearing when we first see her. From there, we took that slightly tomboyish, feisty young thing to the full weight of royalty at her cousin Théodred's funeral, clothing her in layer upon layer of rich, regal fabric. Veils, jewelery and a crown completed an ensemble that was redolent with age and ritual.

"In contrast with Arwen, I used warmer colors and natural fabrics (wools, hessians, velvets and brocades) so that you could feel as if you could reach out and touch her, unlike the more illusive Elves.

"I spent a long time perfecting sleeve lengths and necklines, but this enabled Miranda to find Éowyn within her. I remember watching her put on this huge green velvet number and seeing her sheer excitement at feeling beautiful and feeling herself take on the personality of Éowyn. As with every character, that is the moment when I get my adrenaline rush."

THE GOLDEN HALL
Color studies
Jeremy Bennett

"These were painted from the floor plans and a couple of drawings of Alan Lee's, as the Golden Hall hadn't been built at that stage. I did them for VFX Effects Consultant Mark Stetson. There were a couple more of these, but they were just lighting guides for the Director of Photography to have on set when they were lighting the environment, to give them a feel for how it could look."

EDORAS
Color study
Paul Lasaine

"This is a sketch of the first view of Edoras. However, I didn't think it was particularly successful, so I redid it. The approved painting is the same composition, but it's more of a silhouette of Edoras against a yellow morning sky."

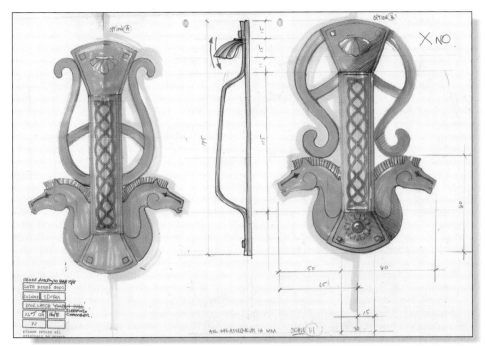

EDORAS
Door knocker designs
Gareth Jensen
Again focusing on the horse motifs so prevalent in and around the Rohirrim culture, these knockers feature on sets built in Edoras. The right-hand version with the inverted horseshoe was the rejected version.

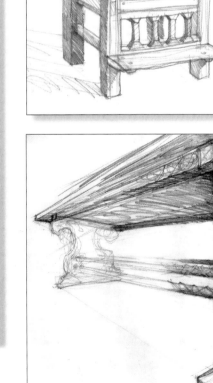

EDORAS
Prop designs
Adam Ellis
A brazier, chair and table designed for the interior of the Golden Hall.

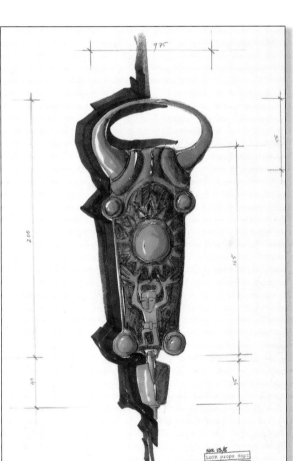

EDORAS
Artifact design
Gareth Jensen
Another major design motif in the Rohan culture is the sun, so here's a small sun icon to go on a wall in Edoras.

THE GOLDEN HALL TAPESTRIES
Tapestry designs
Jeremy Bennett

"These top two are my designs based on reading more about the Rohan culture. The first tapestry is of a famous boar hunt where a king, Folca, was actually skewered by this gigantic boar that had been terrorizing the locals. The second is of Helm Hammerhand, whom Helm's Deep is named after. An interesting character — totally formidable, he was found frozen dead but still standing on the Deeping Wall. It was great to go back and explore what Tolkien had written about this history and then try to recreate it.

"The lower one was adapted from a drawing by Alan Lee that I then took to the color stage for the guys who made the tapestries.

"The illustrations had to be quite simple to translate into large tapestries. The borders were drawn up by Shane Henson — from designs by Alan — and the actual painting was done by Smart Arts, a local contractor, onto a roughly woven canvas. When they came back, a lot of work was done in our textile department to age them down and make them look as though they'd been hanging in a dusty hall for a few hundred years.

"It was an open brief: I could do whatever I wanted — no restrictions. With the paintings, you know exactly what an environment could look like — you've had a brief and it's up to you to realize it and get it to a stage where Peter can say, 'Yeah, that looks like what I imagined.' So in that sense they were a lot of fun."

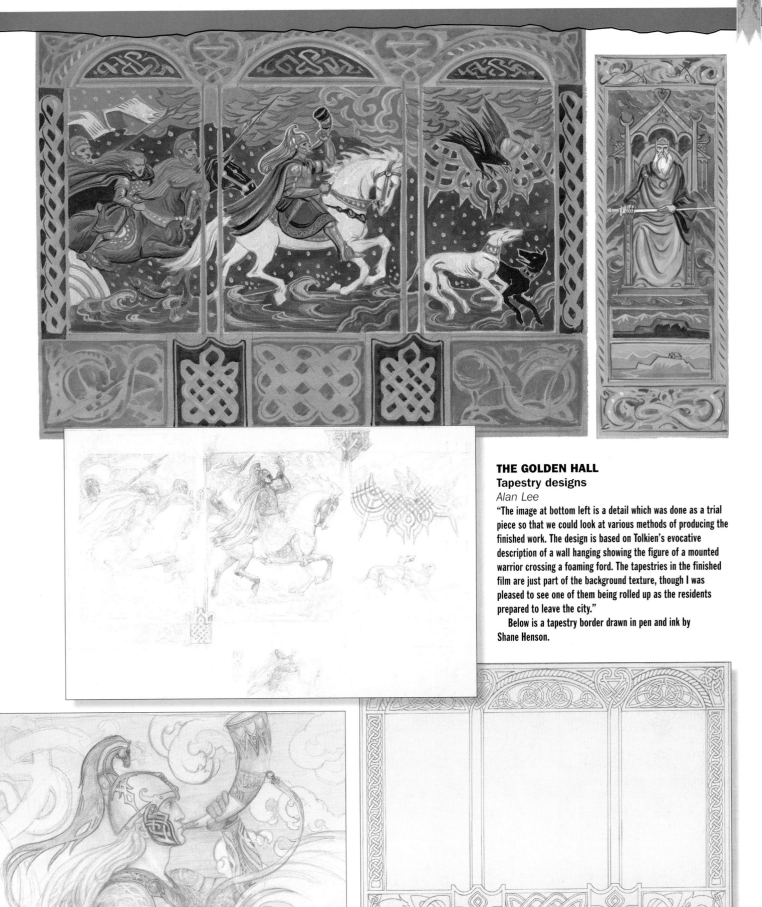

THE GOLDEN HALL
Tapestry designs
Alan Lee

"The image at bottom left is a detail which was done as a trial piece so that we could look at various methods of producing the finished work. The design is based on Tolkien's evocative description of a wall hanging showing the figure of a mounted warrior crossing a foaming ford. The tapestries in the finished film are just part of the background texture, though I was pleased to see one of them being rolled up as the residents prepared to leave the city."

Below is a tapestry border drawn in pen and ink by Shane Henson.

EDORAS
BUILDINGS
Pencil sketches/digital artwork
Alan Lee

"We found the most wonderful location for the city of Edoras in the mountains west of Christchurch. We built the Golden Hall, the stables and a few other buildings on the top of the hill, and a complex of buildings around the gatehouse at the bottom. The wall and the rest of the city were created digitally by Cory Bedwell and others in postproduction. I completed the above image as a guide.

"There are some scenes in the film that take place in bedrooms or antechambers, and these were incorporated into the design of the Golden Hall."

EDORAS STABLES
Pencil sketch
John Howe
"Besides the Golden Hall, it was tempting to imagine a lavishly decorated building for the stables of Edoras. Imagine Sutton Hoo, with an equine twist, and also with a hint of the reverence in which the Rohirrim must hold their horses."

EDORAS STABLES
Pencil sketch
Grant Major
"The stables would have been one of the more important buildings in the city. We thought at one time that we might create a two-story structure for Gandalf's horse, Shadowfax, because of his exalted status as one of the Mearas, having a floor all to himself."

◊ **THE GOLDEN HALL**
Pencil sketch
Alan Lee
"The buildings of Rohan are wooden and based loosely on our idea of structures that would have existed in northern Europe during the Dark Ages. The description of Hrothgar's Hall, Heorot, in the Anglo-Saxon poem <u>Beowulf</u> was probably as useful as Tolkien's own words in evoking the kind of place we wanted to create. We wanted it to feel ancient and strong, bound with iron and heavily decorated. We adopted the sunburst motif as something that felt appropriate for a plains-dwelling, seminomadic people, and, of course, we used lots of carvings of horses on gables and gateways."

EDORAS GATEWAYS ◊
Pencil sketches
Alan Lee
"These studies to the right and below are of the main entrance to Edoras and for a second, smaller gate further into the city. I enjoyed working out the details of the construction of these sets with their various types of locking and barring mechanisms. It was important that everything that we see could have been built a thousand years ago with the materials available to that kind of culture."

▽ **EDORAS**
Pencil sketch
Alan Lee
"The study below is based on my memory of our first, brief visit to the location we were going to use. We had some aerial surveys done so that we could build accurate models of the site before starting construction."

THE GOLDEN HALL
Pencil sketch
Alan Lee

"I did a large number of drawings of this interior, covering it from every angle. We wanted to make it as rich and as authentic as possible. Helen Strevens did a great job on all the drafting and we consulted books on barn construction to make all the timberwork believable. For all its richness, we wanted the first impression to be quite somber, to reflect the state of decay that Saruman and Wormtongue have engendered."

THE GOLDEN HALL
Pencil sketches
Alan Lee

"The drawing below is another version, and very close to an illustration I'd done of Heorot for a book several years earlier. We used weighted ropes on the thatched roofs of our buildings, following examples that we'd seen on farmhouses in remote and equally windswept areas of northern Europe."

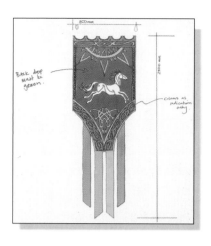

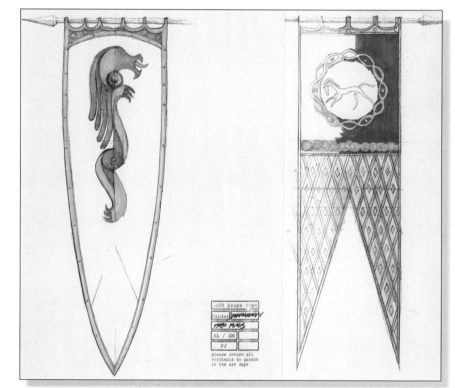

THE GOLDEN HALL
Banner designs
Gareth Jensen

Throughout the rooms and halls of Edoras, a variety
of family heirlooms can be seen as pennants, flags and
tapestries. This is a selection of the designs — all beautifully
executed by fabric artist Lesley Earl-Templeton and a team
of props makers.

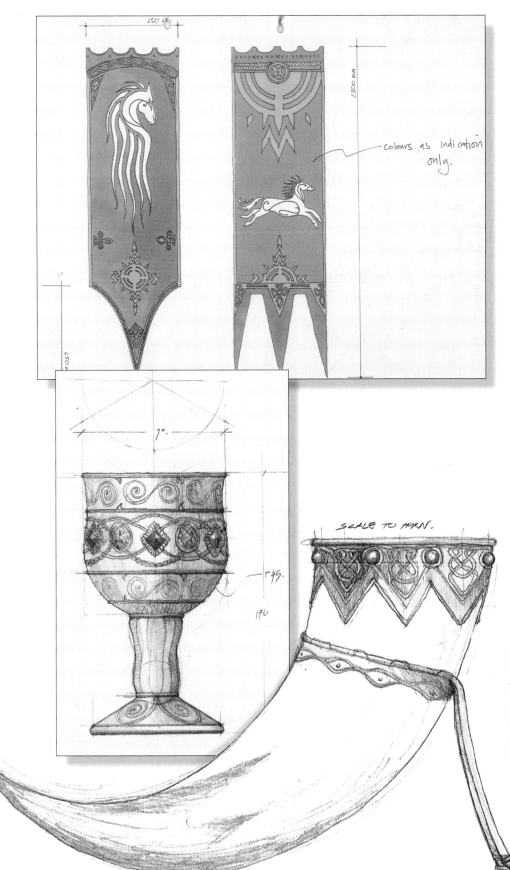

colours as indication only.

SCALE TO HORN.

THE GOLDEN HALL
Drinking vessels
Adam Ellis
The richness of detail that we see in the Rohan architecture, costumes and banners has been carried through to other items that we might find in a royal household. We also made a large number of simpler, everyday items for the refugees and citizens of Edoras.

EDORAS
Saddlery
*Alan Lee
& Gareth Jensen*

"The top horse shows off the full splendor of Théoden's mount. We employed a saddler, Tim Abbot, throughout the production and the numbers and varieties of different types of tack, stirrups and horse armor kept us all busy."

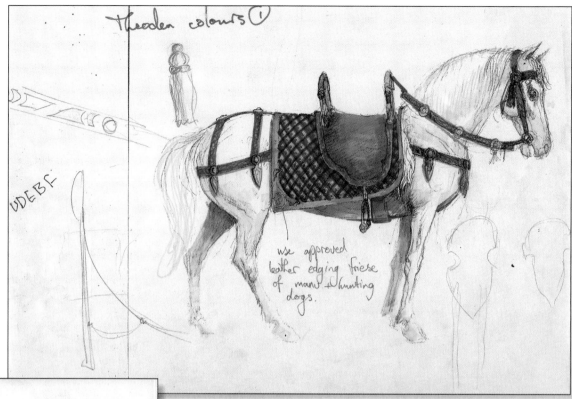

EDORAS
Horse face-plates
Warren Mahy

These three designs were done to assist the leather workers in manufacturing the horse face-plates. Major consideration was given to the comfort of the horse during the process. We had to watch that the cut-outs around the eyes didn't impede the horse's ability to see and that the lower portion of the face-plate kept well away from the horse's nose.

EDORAS
Saddlery
Gareth Jensen

Sketches of the pommel and cantel of Théoden's impressive saddle. The decorative details are representations of the head of Scatha, the great dragon, slain by one of the ancient ancestors of the King of the Mark.

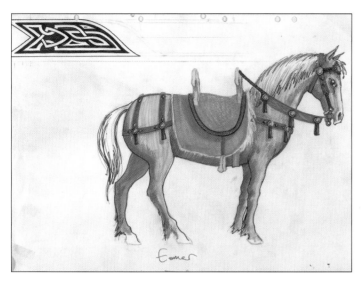

(possible royal guard).

Éomer

EDORAS
Saddlery
Gareth Jensen
The design above was originally for Théodred, but was adapted for use by the Royal Guard at Edoras. The design above left was created for Éomer's horse.

EDORAS
Sketches
Alan Lee
"Some of the different uses we've made of animal motifs. The pencil drawing at top left of this group was for the armrest on Théoden's chair. This would normally have been cast in fiberglass and glued into place, but the carpenter who built the chair was very keen to carve it himself. He made a beautiful job of it. Below it is the running horse design from Théoden's banner, various wooden carvings from around the Golden Hall, and, above, the fountain that Tolkien describes in his account of our heroes' arrival at Edoras."

THE BLACK GATES

◁◁ THE BLACK GATES
Lighting studies
Jeremy Bennett

"These three early lighting studies were completed for the miniatures crew, so they could use these to match the color. I always imagine the land being dead. It's like Mordor is sucking the life out of the atmosphere, out of the air. The lighting is not flat, but it's certainly not warm, and we didn't really want to go for too brutal a look. I think Peter used to say he wanted it to have a sort of tobacco feel, so it's dirty, it's nasty — it's a very tricky environment to handle."

"There was so much detail in the actual gates seen in the film, they're just beautiful things. Anyway, I was blending them back into the atmosphere here — cutting the detail down — to get the feeling of depth. The Easterlings are coming in from the right so you can see the scale,

see how big the Black Gates are meant to be. They're actually about seventy feet, so I cheated the scale so that the environment would look gargantuan.

"We did a lot of drawings for this, an awful lot. It's an environment that's really important to Alan Lee and me. It's the last place in Middle-earth you'd want to be — we had a very clear idea of how we wanted it to look." (To the right is Alan's digital version, blending the real gates with his painting.)

"We wanted to provide a little bit of atmosphere behind the gates themselves — it's there for two reasons. First, to silhouette the gates and play up the beautiful detail there, and second, to allude to the Orc camp which is behind them, to give a feeling of life and movement. This is actually for the tail end of the shot. We start right at the top of the mountains, and tilt down: you have Mount Doom — or the glow of Mount Doom — off to the right-hand side, so that's a major feature in this painting. Until the later part of film three, this is as close as you're going to get to Mordor and Mount Doom itself.

"So it was important to us that it had a very frightening feel — it's daylight, it's not a night shot, but it still needed to look disturbing."

THE BLACK GATES
Digital artwork
Alan Lee

"Two studies to show how the mountainside environment beyond the Easterling army and above the Gate might look."

EASTERLINGS
Design sketches
Johnny Brough (far left) and Warren Mahy (left)

"The great thing about the Easterlings, because they were on the bad side — in an alliance with Sauron — is that you could make them more tribal, they could be a bit more raw and a bit more savage. I loved the idea of having exposed skin, a bare chest — he's almost tempting you: 'Come on! I'm armored to a point, but you know, my heart is open! Just try it!'"

EASTERLING
Pencil sketch
Sourisak Chanpaseuth

"I really went off at a tangent for this one. I think it was just a wild idea at the time — a lot of movement, but I gave him the appearance of being like an assassin, a ninja. With a bit of a samurai look about him, too."

EASTERLINGS
Color sketches
Daniel Falconer

"Sourisak did a great drawing [previous page] that included a fantastic helmet with the silhouette of two really big blades coming out of it, which Peter Jackson really, really liked. So I began trying different helmet designs that would employ that silhouette. It was something that none of the other races that we'd designed at that stage had. The look of the armor itself had been pretty much locked down and we also had a very strong idea of what the color palette would be — ochres, reds, browns, black and brass. The larger image here is a further exploration of the helmet design. Peter liked the shape, he thought it had quite an unusual look — especially the undercut. The final design, which we see in the top right picture, was a combination of this helmet and Sourisak's, his silhouette mixed with the overall shape of mine. And a more open face-guard."

EASTERLING
Color sketch
Warren Mahy

"This is one of the first Easterling designs. I think the first few days we just tried to bring out iconic shapes and colors. I can't remember who started it, but the idea came up of having interlacing panels of plates — similar to Japanese armor, but being metal instead of leather or laminated wood to give them a different shape. Definitely more Middle Eastern than European. There was quite a discussion over the crescent-shaped details on the helmet to ensure that it wasn't too obviously inspired by our own cultures."

EASTERLING
Pencil sketch
Daniel Falconer

"This was one of the earliest Easterling sketches done. I was drawing upon what I thought Easterlings would look like as related in Tolkien's text and I came away with the impression that they were a desert people, quite fearsome. I used a lot of Bedouin and Saharan influences in designing their outfits. In this case I think some of the source material was showing through a little too strongly. It also used the upward-facing lames of armor, which sprang from a drawing that John Howe had done of Ringwraith armor. The Ringwraiths are all kings of various different groups of men and so I thought, 'One of them is probably an Easterling, and as it's a really strong image, why don't we adopt that into the Easterling armor?'"

EASTERLINGS
Color sketches
Daniel Falconer

"At this stage, we were trying to establish very strong iconic features for the Easterlings to differentiate them from the other armies, so one of the things that I played with was that they used different metals in their armor — brass, bronze, coppers. The kind of metals that we haven't seen a lot of in the various other armies, together with new shapes. In this case, I thought it would be interesting to add a strong geometric element to their design, so I used lots of squares and circles. The one below on horseback has a square shield which I liked a lot. They actually didn't ride horses in the finished film, but I know that in parts of the books they're described as being horseback warriors.

"The large picture was getting much closer to the final design. This introduces the idea that they're actually quite a rich culture, and that each warrior wears the badges of his office and the wealth of his family all over him. They would festoon themselves with either war trophies that they've taken off people they've killed or family heirlooms. He's absolutely covered in this sort of stuff. The pattern for the armor is fairly close to what we finally went with, but there were a few changes. Peter felt that we needed a helmet, whereas this one has a turban. He believed that a helmet makes him much more warriorlike and again less obviously from any recognizable culture, which brings us to the drawing at the bottom right of the page.

"He's wearing something between a helmet and a desert mask, and carries a bow with some really large arrows, too. We liked the idea that they had extremely large longbows, almost like the old Japanese ones, although this was dropped in the film."

EASTERLING
Color sketch
Ben Wootten

"I came in after the initial round of drawings had been done, so there was already a direction that Pete liked. The heavy-lamed look, the buildup of lots of small lames. He liked the sharp shapes. And he liked the Eastern feel. So it was basically just exploring some of those options — try some other shapes for the lames — and exploring the directions that Pete liked. Going through a lot of the Oriental books I noticed that indigo blue is a color they wear quite a lot. In the book the Easterlings are described as wearing gold and red, which are really easy colors to pick out highlights on, so I just gave them another color that they might wear underneath their gold and red — a pigment that might work well in a desert."

EASTERLINGS
Color sketch
Warren Mahy

"The sketch below was later down the track. Pete had liked some of what Dan and Ben had done and so we all started adding in little bits and pieces — I favored lots of colored cloth rather than heavy armor. The covered face gives it a Middle Eastern look."

EASTERLING ◊
Color sketch
Sourisak Chanpaseuth

"The designs are based on Daniel's drawing that we spun off into a different direction. All those sharp edges on it are because Peter seems to like the majority of the bad dudes to look as aggressive as possible. I like this skeletal-looking face-plate he has on here. It gives him a 'dead' look. We tried to cover their faces as much as possible."

THE BLACK GATES
Pencil sketches
John Howe

"The Black Gates are quite precisely described by Tolkien, with their flanking towers, the wall across the Isenmouth, and triple gates. Initially, I began with more conventional gates, under arches that are distinctly Númenorean in design, but Peter wanted something he could march his army of thousands through without changing formation. Suddenly the gates became eighty yards across! Sets of wheels were added, and a system with two arcs of inner walls for huge trolls chained to immense beams, who would provide the leverage necessary to open them.

"Peter wanted the wheels that carry the weight of the doors to be visible. A bit unusual from a defensive point of view, but surely clearer to the viewer. The top of each gate tower is part of the same structure and swivels with the gates themselves."

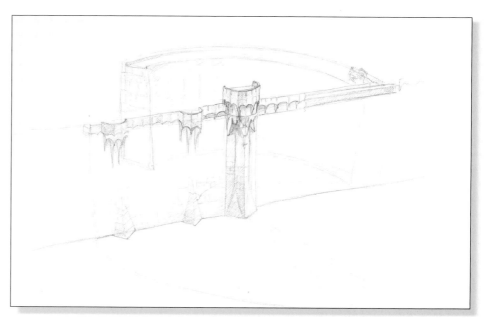

THE BLACK GATES
Pencil sketches
John Howe

"Númenorean architecture is quite arrogant really, but with supple lines inherited from their maritime past which break up the bulkiness of the structures. Only a lack of time stopped me from exploring this avenue all the way back to Númenor itself.

"I am not a huge fan of 'designer's dream' architecture and cities. Too many created fantasy realms look like they are the work of one architect (which is evidently true, but beside the point), a fault born of our contemporary desire to design novel cities and environments, forgetting that any urban area is as much a product of chance as of design. I'm influenced as much by the terrain, the materials used, as by the draftsman's pencil. I tried to bring this to mind when imagining these great structures."

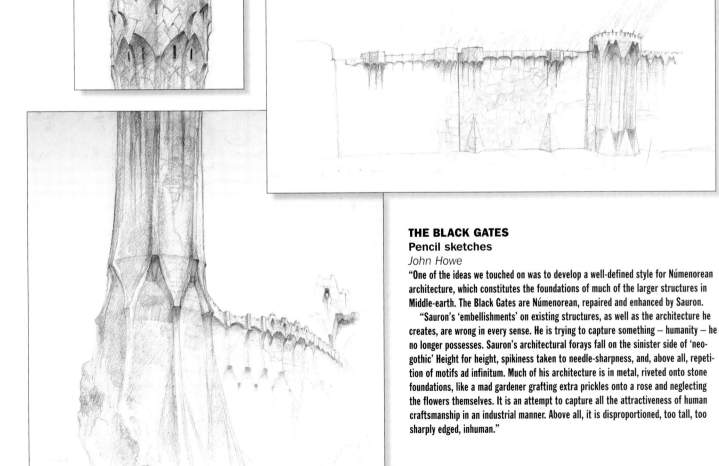

THE BLACK GATES
Pencil sketches
John Howe

"One of the ideas we touched on was to develop a well-defined style for Númenorean architecture, which constitutes the foundations of much of the larger structures in Middle-earth. The Black Gates are Númenorean, repaired and enhanced by Sauron.

"Sauron's 'embellishments' on existing structures, as well as the architecture he creates, are wrong in every sense. He is trying to capture something – humanity – he no longer possesses. Sauron's architectural forays fall on the sinister side of 'neo-gothic' Height for height, spikiness taken to needle-sharpness, and, above all, repetition of motifs ad infinitum. Much of his architecture is in metal, riveted onto stone foundations, like a mad gardener grafting extra prickles onto a rose and neglecting the flowers themselves. It is an attempt to capture all the attractiveness of human craftsmanship in an industrial manner. Above all, it is disproportioned, too tall, too sharply edged, inhuman."

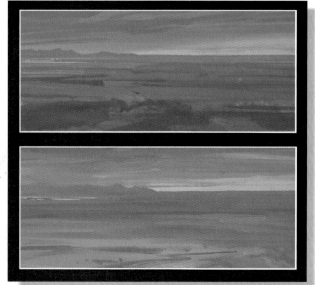

⌂ DAGORLAD PLAINS
Color studies
Jeremy Bennett
"These quick studies show the view from the gates over the Dagorlad Plains and the Dead Marshes that Frodo, Sam and Gollum have just traversed. You have a bit of the Emyn Muil on the left side, and then there are hundreds of miles of nothing — just a desolate plain. These were a rough guide for the matte painter, who then created the scene. We used a cyclorama taken of the Laragahoe Desert for the ground plain and the sky was added later — but it actually has a similar feel to this. I really wanted to keep the low cloud cover that's coming from over our heads. It's just hanging there so you do get a looming atmosphere of death."

THE BLACK GATES ◊
Digital artwork
Yanick Dusseault & Max Dennison
"Our goal was to evoke massive scale — K2-size but without the snow! The solution was to overlay layers of cloud. The painting blends into the miniature while the camera pans down to a full-scale rock set."
"A difficult environment to produce as we are right under Mordor's front door. The color palette was critical: we had to make the lighting bright enough to see the characters but dark enough so that the oppressiveness of the area was tangible. We worked closely with the Art Department, and Compositor Colin Alway was invaluable in pulling all the elements together."

⇨ THE BLACK GATES
Digital artwork
Max Dennison
"The view outside the gates is in essence one heroic painting which covered an angle of about 120 degrees. This view had to give the impression of the blasted devastation, rubble and aridity of the Dagorlad Plains, and establish the distance between us and Emyn Muil off in the distance. A mixture of scenic elements were used in this instance whereas the sky was painted. This and the image to the right were used in multiple shots."

◊ THE BLACK GATES
Digital artwork
Alan Lee

"This was done to position the miniature behind the blue-screen foreground and to show where Gollum might be placed as he watches the Easterling Army approaching the Black Gates. I loved John Howe's designs for the Black Gates and wanted to preserve their gigantic scale. To the right of that is a black-and-white version showing the mountains looming above them."

ROHAN

◊◊ **ROHAN**
Color study
Paul Lasaine
This color study was done to show the
first panoramic view of the Plains of
Rohan, seen by Aragorn, Legolas and Gimli
as they pursue the captured hobbits.

ROHAN
Color study
Paul Lasaine
This was an early design for the sequence
when the Rohan refugees flee Edoras as
it's being burned to the ground during
a Warg attack. This village was built
at Poolburn, in the South Island, and
its fleeing inhabitants were recruited
locally. Just below is a frame of what was
finally shot.

ÉOMER
Color sketches
Warren Mahy

"For Éomer I wanted a royal type of armor — something that was a little more fitting for a prince from the top family. This was unusual for me — I'd never been a drawing-in-color person. I only started doing them when I came to Weta, but I watched Dan with his marker pens. It was good training, because you could start playing with color quickly by photocopying your drawing, playing around with it. 'Ooh, I've done something terrible!' So you just throw it away and then color up another photocopy.

"Éomer's shield was done at the same time as we did Théoden's shield [below]. It's a similar concept, using the same sort of shapes but a little more flamboyantly, probably even to the stage where it was not actually practical."

THÉODEN'S SHIELD
Sketch
Warren Mahy

"The design for the outside was pretty much as is, and the boss — which was Daniel Falconer's idea — was put into the center. The center is surrounded by a ring of galloping horses and these are enclosed within a sunburst."

ÉOMER
Color sketch
Daniel Falconer

"We did not do that many drawings for Éomer. We'd already nailed the Rohirrim look — and Théoden and Éowyn were already well on the way in drawings. I think the Rohan royal guards had been designed and locked off at that stage, so when it came to Éomer, we decided that we would reuse quite a few elements from other armor designs and give them his own flavor. We weren't starting from scratch; we were simply building on what we'd already established.

"This drawing is the image that was approved by Peter. There are small changes that were made — his armor in this case is green, and we made it brown in the end — although, interestingly enough, a green version of it was used for Théodred, when that character was written back into the script later on. The helmet is the same as that used in the final armor. And, of course, the horse emblem is there. It has the white horse tail flowing off the back of his head.

"Again, as much as possible, we would take descriptions as they were in the book and incorporate them into what we were creating. Certainly if there was a description, we'd follow it as much as possible. One little feature that he's got is the pop-up cheek guards, which I thought might give him quite an interesting silhouette — set him apart from the other riders. We don't actually ever see him in the film with them up like that, but they were designed to be able to do so."

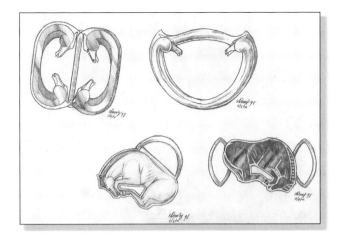

ROHIRRIM
Pencil sketches
Warren Mahy

"As with all things Rohan, the horse motif runs through everything, including buckles. The body armor was really interesting, because it was done in under half a day. Richard Taylor wanted something that they could build for the Rohan extras that would be iconic. It didn't necessarily need to be in leather, but we thought that if it's going to be light, for foot soldiers or for horsemen, leather is going to be more along the lines of what the Rohirrim would make.

"The swords were easy — the one on the left ended up being the generic Rohan sword while the one on the right was just an early concept. Again, it has the horses curving underneath.

"I think that Pete said that the helmet's nose-guard looked — well, let's just say like something a little flaccid! Usually when you try to get a consistent design, an iconic sense of an army, you use geometric shapes or colors. I like the fact that we were able to use horses so much, but I guess that was Tolkien's idea and we ran with it."

RIDERS OF ROHAN

D. Falconer 97
Deta

Erkenbrand:

"...Amid them strode a man tall and strong. His shield was red. As he came to the valley's brink, he set to his lips a great black horn and blew a ringing blast..."

ROHIRRIM
Color sketch
Daniel Falconer

"This is one of the earliest Rohan drawings — and we hadn't really established a good look for them yet. This one's quite Norse; it's also quite heavy and clunky. At this stage on the job, none of us had done much research into the armor yet; it wasn't until John Howe and Alan Lee turned up that we really learned how armor works. John in particular is an expert on medieval armor, and was able to educate us in the do's and don'ts of armor construction and design. I think the armor took a huge step forward in quality after he joined us and was able to bring that depth of knowledge to it.

"Ultimately this drawing didn't really yield us anything that we finally went with. Although the color scheme that's presented here is something that stayed much the same — the strong grass greens that Tolkien talks about the Rohirrim having. This was a character, Erkenbrand, who was said to carry a red shield. I don't think we actually ever see Erkenbrand or hear him mentioned by name in the film at all, but at this stage we didn't have a script to work from, we only had the books."

ROHIRRIM
Pencil sketch
Daniel Falconer

"Pete said early on that he didn't want all the Rohirrim to have the same uniform armor which, for example, the Gondorians do, simply because they're a far-flung people spread across the broad landscape of Rohan. They're farmers and herdsmen, and when they are called together to fight to defend their land, they won't all have exactly the same armor. They have armor that they've put together over the years. It has a certain style that's universal, but there was still a lot of room for actually designing individuals to be quite distinct from each other, as long as they stayed within the established stylistic look. The main sketch is of an old soldier — weary, and probably a little big for his armor."

ROHIRRIM
Pencil sketches
Warren Mahy

"These were done before Pete started signing off on anything. We liked the idea that there was fabric in the designs, that they tended to be more Nordic-looking as far as having the long, long shirts, with chainmail underneath.

"I was trying to keep it simple enough — especially with the fabric — so that we could put a fabric cloak over the top of a piece of armor, or another piece of clothing that had a little piece of chainmail on the bottom to give a layered effect."

WARG RIDERS
Pencil sketch
Warren Mahy

"This was an idea for Sharkû rather than a generic Warg rider. I wanted him to look tribal in the sense of fur and bone. I always thought that the Wargs were bred in Mordor from stocks of different animals or doglike wolves, and the Warg riders actually were part of the training crew as well — even to the point where they became one with the Warg they rode, so these guys would live with them and feed them. I always liked the idea that the Wargs were intelligent enough to have their own language. The fact is, if it chose to, a Warg could just as easily turn on the rider . . ."

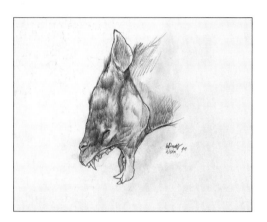

WARG
Pencil sketch
Warren Mahy

"A very early idea for a Warg head. Note that the eye is down by the mouth. Eventually it moved a little bit higher, but stayed forward, and the jawbone goes way back into the head."

WARG
Pencil sketch
Sourisak Chanpaseuth

"I based these on pit bull dogs. I was trying to get away from the typical wolf-look of the Warg. Richard Taylor suggested it could be almost ratlike, so this was the result."

WARG RIDERS
Pencil sketches
Christian Rivers

"These are two unfinished Sharkû designs. When you're designing armor it's very easy to take shortcuts, and say, 'Oh, this bit's leather!' — and then just draw a boring piece of flat leather. However, Richard Taylor wanted to ensure that we were all going to design pieces so that when the camera is close up on this creature, you look at the intricate detail and it looks like something that someone's spent months over. And in an ugly way, obviously, because they're Orcs. No beautiful patterning, just a layer of leather with bone stitched over with fur, and then another piece stitched on for support that's worn away, and then another piece stitched back on . . . This thing has probably been worn for years and been repaired and damaged and repaired again. So they needed to be different from the ordinary armored Orcs. If anything, we tried to give the Warg riders an almost organic feel. I mean, although the Wargs are powerful, you wouldn't want to load them down with too much metal — otherwise the Wargs wouldn't go very fast.

"We wanted Sharkû to be the baddest, fiercest, nastiest looking of the Warg riders, as he's the one who's been around the Wargs the most. So the obvious thing is to give him horrific scarring, and Pete took that to the extreme when we actually put on the makeup. He wanted a few plates that locked his skull back together. It just gives him an even nastier look.

"The shoulder piece in the near right sketch was starting to look a bit too like shoulder pads. A bit Mad Max-ish. A little too what we call 'overdesigned.'"

WARG RIDERS
Pencil sketch
Christian Rivers

"This was probably one of the more cohesive kinds of armor designs. I'd done it as a full uniform, so you have all these elements that are coming through: the fur cape, the helmet (similar to a lot of designs that Warren Mahy did, which then became quite standard for the Orcs), a little flying helmet thing with an eye-guard with spikes coming off to enhance the ferocity. It also gives the impression, subconsciously, of hair being blown back and therefore helps reinforce the sense of speed these creatures move at; having someone ride with all his hair hanging down doesn't look like they're moving fast, but with all these sharp angles you really believe that these guys are flying along!"

WARG RIDERS
Pencil sketch
Warren Mahy
"This was the first rider I did — the Warg is just a mastiff, basically. A big, big mastiff, with a weird back. I was trying to get more of a horse feel into it, but it's starting to look a bit more reptilian as well."

WARG RIDERS
Pencil sketch
Warren Mahy
"This is one of my earliest illustrations — in fact it's one that I sent to Richard Taylor to begin with, before I was even on the project. It's more cartoonlike. It was when I was looking for work, so I certainly didn't know what Peter Jackson wanted."

WARG RIDERS
Pencil sketch
Warren Mahy

"This was a later version of Sharkû. There was an illustration that Johnny Brough did which had quite a high back to the leather armor, and Pete quite liked it, so we started adding that in. This is pretty much the starting point for the final costume design. You can see that he's carrying a piece of meat for his Warg. Nice."

WARG SADDLES
Color designs
Warren Mahy

"These are schematics for the saddles, the idea being that it was a jockey saddle, where the Warg rider's feet moved quite far back and he leaned forward over the Warg's shoulder."

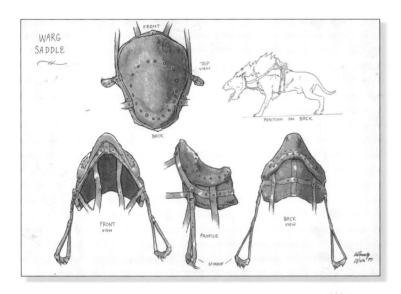

WARG RIDERS
Pencil sketch
Christian Rivers

"This is an early idea for a Warg rider. Originally it was just a concept design for the Orc Grishnákh, done in about 1999. I was trying out the look of the face. We'd made a few sculptures of Orcs and at this stage Grishnákh was going to be one of the Moria Orcs, when they weren't so distinctively different from the Goblins. So I had a few things, like the mummified Dwarf jawbone hanging around his neck, with the beard still attached, which was a nasty piece of desecration — something to make him deeply offensive to Gimli. Although I was trying to come up with a character design — and anyway this drawing would have been difficult to accomplish in prosthetics — Grishnákh looks nothing like this in the finished film!"

WARG RIDERS
Pencil sketches
Warren Mahy

"At the beginning Pete used a few words that were helpful to us — it was a guide to what he was looking for — he liked the idea of the Wargs being almost reptilian but prehistoric as well. The direction that the main sketch was going in was definitely more doglike. It was more mastiff but strange — with bad anatomy as well! Then it started drifting more toward a prehistoric doglike creature, only with weird bends and stretches.

"Of these other pictures the one to the right on this page was one that Peter liked and suggested went toward the final design. The idea being that it had a longer neck than a normal dog — almost the size of a small pony — eyes quite forward on the face and the ears way back. There's quite a mound on the back of its skull and a lot of muscle, making it almost hyenalike. There was also an idea at the beginning that they had a muzzle across their face, not necessarily as armor but maybe just following on from the idea that the riders have lost a few hands in the training process.

"The one at the top of this page is much less doglike and has lost its nose, which Pete liked — it didn't happen in the end, though. The Wargs actually had a thumb on their front limbs so that they could hold on to something — not necessarily to manipulate it, but so they could get up a wall, for example, by grabbing and pulling themselves up.

"The two smaller sketches are ones that we went backward and forward with a few times before they were eventually dropped. I was trying to bring in more of a horse feel into the face of the left-hand one, while the other one goes back to the dog origins."

WARGS
Maquettes
Warren Mahy
These maquettes were created by Weta to show the CGI designers how the Wargs looked in terms of size and weight.

◊ WARGS
Color guides
Warren Mahy

"There wasn't much discussion with Pete about colors. He basically just said, 'Come up with something!' The idea was to go pretty much from wolf colors through to the African wild dog. I was playing around with those colors — tans, oranges — and I did have quite a lot of white in these guys as well, around their lower legs, and around the chin. This detail appears in the final version together with more tan. Unfortunately, there's not so much of these patterned colors in evidence. I actually like the initial concept that there was a lot harder patterning to them, blotches round the back, tiger stripes, etc., but there you go . . ."

EAST WALL OF ROHAN
Color studies
Jeremy Bennett

"Here are two studies of an Uruk-hai on a rock. The camera pans round to the left to reveal the Uruk camp. They're on the Rohan Plains, there's the moon off in the distance, but the valley is completely misted out. Pete wanted to get a feeling for what we might see — or what we might not see. In the final shot we do have more of a feeling of a horizon, there are some rocky features coming through, but color-wise it's very similar to these except there's just a little more detail in the foreground."

RIVENDELL

110 The Art of THE TWO TOWERS

Final matte painting
Yanick Dusseault
"This painting was done in a
more monochromatic palette,
to convey a slight nostalgic
feeling to the sequence."

ARWEN
**Costume design
sketches**
Ngila Dickson
"The additional pickup scenes that
we filmed allowed me to design
some wonderful new costumes for
Arwen, in much richer colors than
we had seen her wearing in the
first film. As with some of the first
film's designs, I used light silks
and dark colors, the latter suiting
both the Rivendell Elf look and
Liv's own coloring. Some of the
designs here are for outfits that
Arwen wears in visions of her as
Aragorn's queen, including one at
the bottom of the facing page,
which she wears at his funeral. Of
course, these are all just things
that may come to pass — nothing's for certain until we see
film three!"

◁ DEAD KING ARAGORN
Color study/digital artwork
Jeremy Bennett/Gus Hunter
"The painting below was used as a rough compositional guide for miniatures as well as a lighting study for set. Once the live action and miniatures were shot we combined these elements together and replaced the sky to show what they might look like for postproduction."

RIVENDELL
Color scheme
Jeremy Bennett

"Here I've taken the miniature and relit it along with its environment, attempting to capture the melancholic atmosphere which permeates Rivendell at this stage of the film. This was then used as a guide for the miniatures team to work from."

RIVENDELL
Matte painting layouts
Gus Hunter

The smaller painting is for the background behind Arwen and Aragorn during a romantic scene at dusk, which Yanick Dusseault based his final matte painting on. The bigger painting was completed for when Aragorn is about to leave Rivendell in the early morning, and Max Dennison based his final matte painting on this layout.

RIVENDELL
Miniature and digital artwork
Alan Lee
"This is a design for a matte painting, which utilizes the miniature of Rivendell [top] that was created in the Weta Workshop."

ISENGARD

◊◊ ISENGARD
Environment and massive study
Gus Hunter

This is an early concept to show what the Uruk-hai troops and background environment cyclorama might look like as they leave Isengard.

ORCS
Sketches
Christian Rivers

"The guy with no leg on the right — I think that may have started life as a design for Grishnákh's armor, actually, but it's basically Orc armor. But for a featured Orc rather than a background Orc, so he had to look a little different. More complete. I was trying to give him quite a cohesive armor design — the Orcs' armor is, obviously, bits and pieces — a bit of chainmail here or a bit of platemail here — and basically cobbled together. So I wanted to give him, without giving him a nice neat suit, a few odds and ends but still make it look like a full suit of armor. Trying to incorporate a lot of sharp curves, nasty spiked corners, so when you saw him in this army, he'd stick out from the background Orcs.

"The bigger figure on the left was just a generic design that really wasn't for anyone in particular. And again, as you can see, it's all cobbled together — just a chainmail vest, and then he's got bits of fur and leather wrapped around his shoulders and stuff — basically pulling together various bits and pieces. These were the only Orcs to be specifically designed for <u>The Two Towers</u> rather than reusing Orcs from the first film, because of the Wargs. We were incorporating a lot more fur and spiky manes down the back of their armor. Basically, they're designed so that they look as if they're part of the Warg — you see them as a striking silhouette across the distance. This one's quite an early design from what I remember — because, I mean, at this stage they hadn't started making any armor and weapons yet. They hadn't actually started constructing any, so we were trying to sort of just come up with concepts to then give to the armor designers and then they'd take that and run with it in their own way — because they obviously know a lot more about the materials that they're using and have a lot more knowledge of the craft of stitching leather together and actually manufacturing these pieces of armor than we do when we draw them."

ORCS
Sketches
Sourisak Chanpaseuth

"These are some designs for one of the Hero Orcs. Peter wanted ideas for these featured Orcs. I knew we'd see the costumes a bit closer on screen, so these are really, really delicate. You can see each bit of armor and costume in really fine details on screen."

ORC AND ORC DAGGERS
Sketches
Warren Mahy

"This guy is a very early Orc — he might have even been done when we were doing Goblin armor, before we stopped calling them Goblins. When we were doing the Goblins — or when we were doing the Orcs later — designs sometimes crossed over between all three — Uruk armor became Orc armor and so on. I based this armor on the fact that it's probably made up from stuff that they've stolen, little bit of Elven cloth here, Dwarf armor there . . . Gondorian studded leather and all that.

"And it has these upward sort of spikes as well — the idea being they were either sharpened bits of wood or bits of metal — something that's still functional, but practical. And offensive. Then I had to design their weaponry. Goblin daggers — the one he's carrying has the traditional sort of Orc pollem on it, except that there's a bit of a guard underneath the head. I then did a variety of different dagger ideas because someone was always running up and saying 'Okay — this character needs a dagger! We need to get him a dagger now!' So I was always running up quick ideas."

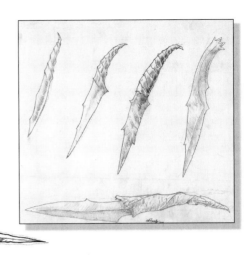

ORCS
Sketches
Ben Stenbeck

More early designs for prominent Orcs in the battle scenes, with the spiked backs and necks to their armor again reflecting possible linkage to the Wargs. The one with a hood was designed as an Orc blacksmith, working in the pits to create swords and daggers.

⬙ ISENGARD
Color study
Jeremy Bennett

"This is a scene that I was not sure would be appearing in the film, so it was really just done to give a feeling for what the valley might look like. At this stage the Orcs have totally deforested Isengard — I probably need to give it a lot more stumps and things in there — it's totally devastated, and I really just wanted to make it look windswept, almost like there was a squall passing through. And you just have the guys sort of coming through into the foreground — just walking on by."

ISENGARD
Color studies
Paul Lasaine
"The two smaller pictures were done as an Isengard before-and-after comparison. The idea was to show how the Isengard valley looked at the beginning of the saga [far left] before we find out that Saruman is actually the bad guy and what later becomes of the valley after Saruman comes under the spell of Sauron [left]."

ORTHANC TOWER
Saruman on balcony
Laurent Ben-Mimoun & Charlie Tait
Here Laurent's matte paintings have been composited by Charlie
into the final spectacular shot.

ORTHANC TOWER
Color study
Jeremy Bennett
"This is the very last frame of a shot
where you pull out to reveal . . . this!
We start on the balcony with Saruman
and Wormtongue, and there's this
elaborate pullout from the tower right
over the sea of Uruks. This painting was
really just a guide to look at pike placement, and to give a general feeling to
the environment behind Isengard — it's
early morning light, but quite moody."

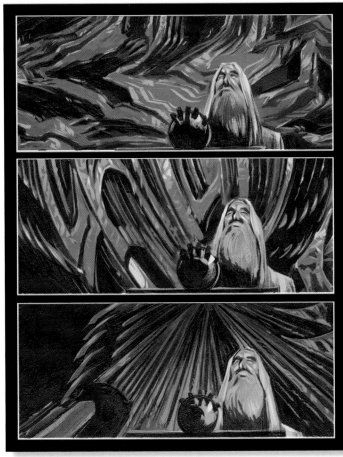

⌂ SARUMAN'S NIGHTMARE
Concept

Jeremy Bennett

"When these were done, we weren't sure that we would have a prologue sequence in
<u>The Fellowship of the Ring</u> where Sauron was revealed (we thought he may be saved for
<u>The Return of the King</u>). So I wanted to just hide him in the architecture in the background
to such a degree that you might see the film three times and not notice anything — and someone might say, 'I think I saw something in the walls — was it Sauron's face?'

"At this point Saruman's communicating with Sauron. He thinks he has it all under
control — he can use the palantír correctly — but in actual fact, Sauron has total control
over him. So it's a little obvious, but I think the idea of using the sheen and the detail to
suggest Sauron's presence could have been worthwhile."

⌂ SARUMAN: THE PALANTÍR
Digital artwork

*Jeremy Bennett
& Gus Hunter*

Gus took Jeremy's original painting,
scanned it, and then did the variations
above.

ISENGARD
Storyboard concept
Gus Hunter
The panels to the right are among several that Gus did. This sequence shows a long aerial move into Isengard as Saruman prepares for war.

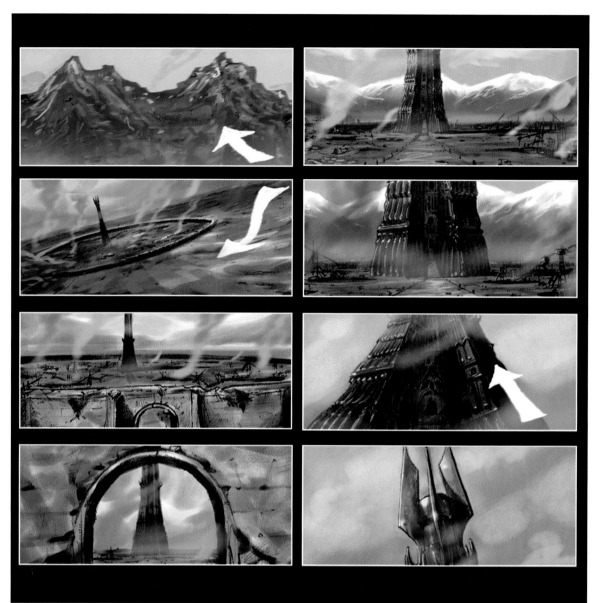

ISENGARD
Color studies
Jeremy Bennett
"The artwork below involves designing a background for the blue-screen shot, and showing the ash-covered desolation of the environment Saruman was creating, contrasted with the glow of his fires from the caverns below, more of which can be seen in the painting opposite."

WARG PITS
Composition and color study
Jeremy Bennett
"This study was done to help the Miniatures Unit create the background complex of caverns and the pit that contained the ferocious, half-starved Wargs. Sharkû awaits his orders."

SARUMAN AND WILD MEN
Composition and color study
Jeremy Bennett
"A quick study to establish the overall composition of the shot, like the position of the Wild Men, number of torches and general amount of smoke and haze. An illustration like this will be used as a fairly good guide for the compositor, who will piece the shot together."

ITHILIEN

◇◇ **ITHILIEN MOONSET**
Digital artwork
Paul Lasaine & Craig Potton
"This is the view of Ithilien from the top of the Henneth Annûn falls. It's a digital painting using photo elements taken by Craig Potton. If it looks somewhat reminiscent of Rivendell, it's because we shot these photos at the same location — the Fox River Valley in North Westland, South Island."

HARADRIM
Colour sketches
Daniel Falconer
"Early on, we devised a look for the Haradrim which Peter quite liked, drawing on influences from Papua New Guinean island cultures mixed in with a bit of African stuff. But what we tried to do was mix them in such a way that it wasn't recognizably any one particular culture from our own world. We tried to create a new culture, but one that was grounded in the same reality as our own. So, we established a look for the Haradrim, but it became apparent that it wasn't quite right — and a bit of rethinking went on. As it developed we started introducing more elements that made them less familiar, and we also added a lot more robes.

"The drawing of a young Haradrim soldier presented a bit of a problem for us; we had created the Haradrim to be this fearsome, quite repugnant warrior race, and we'd done everything that we could to dehumanize them. However, we learned later that there's a scene in which the hobbits come across a young Haradrim soldier who dies horribly, and you're actually supposed to empathize with him. This young guy's nothing much more than a kid. He's been pressed into service and just died horribly for Sauron, who he's terrified of, obviously. He was drawn in an attempt to take our fearsome Haradrim warrior and turn him into a frightened young boy. We softened the design, losing a lot of the jagged edges which we had put on the early Haradrim warriors, so that he would look like he was one of them but audiences could empathize with him more."

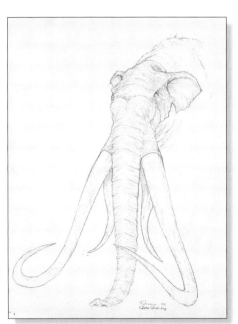

◊ MÛMAK
Pencil sketch
Daniel Falconer

"This particular mûmak was done quite early on, and it was an exploration of the proportions of the face and head. Obviously, these are of an elephant type, but Peter didn't want to just make them an elephant or a mammoth or something that we knew. They were of the same family, but grown to a ridiculous scale — much, much bigger, and a little bit more sinister in appearance. I played around with making the ears smaller, because that makes the head seem larger. Very small eyes, very widely spaced, with a large, powerful brow and a long trunk because, obviously, he's very tall, so he's going to need this to reach down and pick up food."

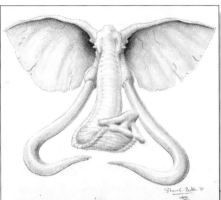

◊ MÛMAK
Pencil sketch
Shaun Bolton

Shaun's drawings (left and below) are more traditionally elephantine but with really vicious tusks, although opting for just two rather than Daniel's four.

◻ MÛMAK
Pencil sketch
John Howe

"Of course the mûmakil can't be just oversized elephants . . . I was very much taken with the idea that many of the evil creatures in Sauron's armies are not just dumb beasts goaded into combat, but purposeful monsters bent on destruction."

ITHILIEN
Color schemes
Jeremy Bennett

"The top one was a first pass at the moon setting, where Faramir and Frodo are observing it over Ithilien. The second version is fairly close to the finished matte painting, incorporating Peter's feedback regarding the overall composition."

⇨ ITHILIEN
Digital artwork
Alan Lee

"Placing Númenorean ruins into Middle-earth."

ITHILIEN ▷
Color study
Paul Lasaine
This is one of a series
of paintings that Paul
did to explore different
color schemes for
the sky.

◁ **HENNETH ANNÛN**
Compositional study
Gus Hunter & Yanick Dusseault
Gus has replaced the blue screen behind Faramir and
Frodo with Yanick's matte painting and altered it slightly
to establish the composition for this shot.

▽ **HENNETH ANNÛN**
Matte painting
Gus Hunter & Deak Farrand
Deak completed an initial matte painting of the waterfall,
which Gus altered per Peter's brief.

FARAMIR
Costume design sketches
Ngila Dickson

"Although there is the family connection between Faramir and his brother, Boromir, this costume is much closer to that of Aragorn. Both of these characters are Rangers, and so both costumes needed to be tough yet light, and in colors that would serve them well in avoiding detection — browns and greens. This design allowed for Faramir to have his smaller possessions strapped close to his body. The tunic is quilted for both warmth and protection and the leather has the Tree of Gondor on it. The vambraces are there as a link to Boromir."

HENNETH ANNÛN
Color study
Paul Lasaine

This painting shows the interior of the cave where Faramir and the Ithilien Rangers have their hideout. The waterfall which pours into the Forbidden Pool creates a curtain that obscures the occupants from view.

⬨ **THE FORBIDDEN POOL**
Color study
Jeremy Bennett
"This shows a color palette for the scene where Gollum is caught by the Ithilien Rangers while he is fishing. It's Frodo's point of view as he peers over the edge of the cliff and we see Gollum dive into the pool and emerge with a fish."

⬨ **THE FORBIDDEN POOL**
Pencil sketch
Alan Lee
"We built the set for the pool and the interior of the cave in the same studio so that they could share the waterfall which Ed Mulholland's construction crew made for us. In the final shots more water was composited into the scene to make it feel more natural."

⬨ **THE FORBIDDEN POOL**
Pencil sketch
Alan Lee
"There is a scene where Faramir and his Rangers spot Gollum frollicking around and hunting for fish in a pool at the foot of Henneth Annûn, which is a crime punishable by death, so they get Frodo to come and investigate. This was one of a couple of shots done with Gollum by the pool."

OSGILIATH
Color study
Jeremy Bennett

"This is a color study of Osgiliath, the once great city of Gondor that straddles the River Anduin. It concentrates mainly on the far side of the river with the emphasis on the miniature set's relationship to the brooding sky."

OSGILIATH
Pencil sketches
Alan Lee

"Osgiliath was one of the most enjoyable sets to work on. We had a lot of existing pieces of masonry left over from some of our earlier sets and added new designs to make the ruins as rich and complex as possible. I thought that the river might have become choked in places and flooded some areas of the city — which adds to the interest. The bird's-eye view shows the broken bridges and an island, somewhat inspired by the Isle de la Cité in Paris, which contains a large cathedral-like building. We know that Osgiliath had once housed one of the Palantírs which had been lost when the tower it was kept in collapsed, so it could be that building."

OSGILIATH
Color studies
Jeremy Bennett

"These were done for the guys working down on the wet set. They built this fantastic Osgiliath set and I was just thinking about the time of day – late afternoon – and what the sun might be doing as it's hitting the set. I quite like the second one down. They are part of a series of pictures that I did to show Peter.

"Some of them are views from the Orc side, at sunset, when they're about to head over en masse on their rafts. I'm using elements that Alan Lee designed – it was quite fun to rearrange them, to play around with the composition.

"The one below is a slightly more finished study than those above of the environment, involving the live-action foreground."

MORDOR MOUNTAINS
Color studies
Jeremy Bennett

"This was maybe one of five quick color studies looking at possible color palettes and giving thought to how the Mordor mountain range would sit behind the miniature."

MORDOR MOUNTAINS
Digital matte paintings
Mathieu Raynault

"This is one of a series of matte paintings that I did for the Dead Marshes sequence. Using the artwork [right] by Jeremy Bennett as a starting point, I established what we needed to see. We knew this painting would end up in a number of shots, serving as a backdrop to Frodo, Sam and Gollum hiding in the Dead Marshes, so it had to be simple in its construction and big enough in resolution to cover three or four different camera angles. My job was to create the sky and the Mordor mountain range. The sky was created using several pictures that I'd taken around Wellington, New Zealand, and the mountains using digital painting techniques.

"At the bottom is a matte painting that was designed as a background to Frodo in the Osgiliath ruins, which shows Mount Mindolluin. I started by painting a rough sketch that was approved by the art directors, and later used a mixture of photographic textures and digital painting to create a believable mountain range and sky."

OSGILIATH
Digital matte paintings
Roger Kupelian

"With the scene above, I had to match a live plate with a very specific set of expectations: Ithilien and Osgiliath, with the River Anduin cutting through the plain, as well as Minas Tirith in the distance. There are no plains this vast in New Zealand so this had to be a painting. Even the miniatures provided had to be completely redressed to suit the feel of the shot. Animation was added as well, both in the sky, lighting effects and minute details within the city, which by themselves are barely noticeable. This rendered sequence, an animated matte painting really, was then handed over to Jon Bowen, who then masterfully combined it with the live plate. Because of the enormity of the area it was replacing, this was among the most difficult matte shots produced for the film."

HELM'S DEEP

◁◇ **HELM'S DEEP**
Color study
Jeremy Bennett
"There's a lot of Uruk-hai — and you see them all. The idea here was that it's nighttime, and they're dressed in black, so you're never going to see them bar the flames of their torches. I wanted to allude to pikes against the night sky, and banners, and fire in the darkness."

HELM'S DEEP ◁
Color study
Paul Lasaine
"This was done as a guide for Alex Funke and the Miniatures Unit to establish the look of the Helm's Deep valley as the Rohan refugees first arrive and make their way to safety."

HELM'S DEEP ▽
Color study
Jeremy Bennett
"Both this painting and the one at the top of the next page were done for mood and atmosphere, and to establish the placement of siege ladders and the digitally created Uruk-hai storming over the walls and up the causeway."

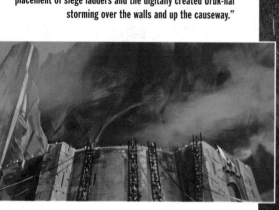

HELM'S DEEP ◇
Color study
Jeremy Bennett
"The vastly outnumbered defenders await the approaching Uruk army, their torches just visible through the gloom and mist. This was done as a guide for Mark Lewis, who composited most of the shots in this dramatic sequence."

ELVEN ARMY
Color sketches
Warren Mahy

"These helmets were created for a sequence in the film that no longer happens, with Arwen appearing with the Elven army that arrives at Helm's Deep, so these were designed for her. They were not too flash but still have a bit of class, as befitting her status."

ELVEN ARMY
Designs
Daniel Falconer

"In early versions of the script Arwen originally had a much bigger role. It called for us to design for her some armor and weaponry — in particular a bow. It was much the same as Legolas' bow, but I drew on a shape that we'd established as an Arwenesque motif for the points of the bow — a star shape, which of course is the Evenstar. I carried that through into a lot of her Elven equipment; her quiver was designed to match the bow. Time and again, we tried to use the same visual cues throughout the various cultures — the look of the Elves was very Art Nouveau. The quiver was built, although we went with a different color scheme. There was a point in the earlier script where she was given some vambraces, and these were not of Elven design but actually Rohan. In the same scene, she would also wear a helmet and possibly some Rohan chainmail, so overrall a Rohan look."

ELVEN ARMY
Color sketch
Warren Mahy

"A very early Elven sword. We began with the idea that Elves used organic shapes, but this evolved as time went on because in battle you wouldn't want so much intricate jewelery adorning your weapon. I got great enjoyment from studying Asian weapons — not just Japanese ones — as I think they tend to look a little bit more elegant; that would have been the kickoff point for this."

ELVEN ARMY
Color sketches
Warren Mahy

"These were actually drawn back in the early days. They are designs to conceptualize the Second Age army led by Gil-galad that appears in the prologue to The Fellowship of the Ring, but in the end the prologue used stuff we'd created for other things so they became a focus again for the Third Age Elven army."

ELVEN ARMY
Color sketches
Daniel Falconer

"The Elven armor that we see in the second film was actually designed before we designed the Elven armor in the first film. The guy on the near right is probably the earliest Elf drawing done. At this stage, we hadn't really locked down the overall look of the three films, so the armor you see was very much more elaborate, Dungeons and Dragons-style armor. The next one [extreme right, facing page] was a bit of a breakthrough for the Elven design — I did this very quick drawing just as a rough study and Peter really responded to the shapes in it. He thought they were very elegant — so this very much ended up being the template that we followed to develop the Elven armor. Eventually this evolved into the picture on the nearer right which became the definitive Elven armor drawing from which we then began building the stuff. Obviously, as we built it, we discovered certain things were impractical, and needed to change: I think the helmet and shoulder guards in particular changed a good deal; and we added a leather under-tunic as well — but other than that, it stayed fairly similar.

"Although traditional Elven costumes are very loose and flowing, in contrast their armor is enclosing. That's because you can't have armor that is hanging off of you; your armor has to be quite tight — it has to defend you so it can't be getting in the way when you're trying to fight. So, while we designed armor that was stylistically interesting and artistic, it always had to conform back to the human body and be functional. There are certain liberties taken for the sake of this being a movie but it had to have the appearance of being practical, so that's why we pulled everything in tight on the body.

"Because the Elves are leaving Middle-earth, we figured that they're saying goodbye. They refer to it as the autumn of their years and as a consequence, because they identify so strongly with the forests of Middle-earth, we used a lot of autumnal tones in their coloring — dried leaves, reds and browns and oranges and bronzes."

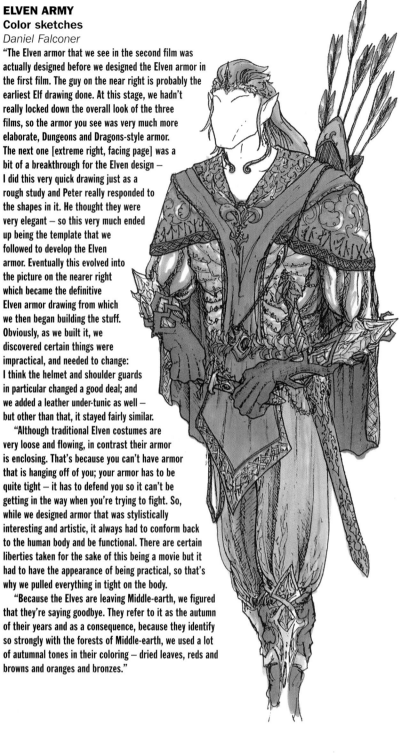

Falconer 98 / Weta Workshop

ELVEN ARMY
Color sketch
Ben Wootten

"This was one of the first sketches done. I used a flowing look so that it looks like a dress of chain-mail, to give the idea of something graceful, something elegant. There was also an early idea of using laminated wood for the armor similar to an oriental theme, different material to represent a different philosophy and to make them quite different from human and Dwarven armors. There's almost a feather motif on the elbow, which is almost represented all the way through, it could be leaves, it could be feathers. And the broad leggings would give freedom of movement and grace and hopefully not inhibit the flow of the actors too much."

ELVEN ARMY
Pencil sketch
Christian Rivers

THE GLITTERING CAVES
Color study
Paul Lasaine

"These are the Glittering Caves, a hiding place behind Helm's Deep for the refugees during the battle. I based most of this on photographs that I had of some caverns in Virginia. I went to see them — they were beautiful. They had no guidebook, but they did have one of those old 3-D View-Master reels. When I came to paint this, I had my wife ship them out to me. So I was sitting there with my 3-D View-Master glasses on. Strange."

THE GLITTERING CAVES
Pencil sketches
John Howe

"Caverns are frustrating things to draw. They are a catalogue of subterranean marvels — assuredly most exquisite to behold, but not exactly stimulating to conceptualize The smaller picture shows the mouth of the major caves. A wide opening, not some discreet passage seemed to convey the weight of the mountain more dramatically."

THE GLITTERING CAVES ◊
Pencil sketch
John Howe

"To the right we have Legolas and Gimli exploring the Glittering Caves. All the stalactites just brush the surface of the water. I wanted to created the feeling of an inverted mineral forest — something that would be pleasing to both of them."

THE GLITTERING CAVES
Pencil sketch
John Howe

"Here is another view of the entrance to the caverns behind Helm's Deep. The unusual element floating in the middle is a leather greave for a Rohan rider. Sometimes you have to sketch while the idea's hot!"

THE GLITTERING CAVES
Pencil sketch
Alan Lee

"We did a number of studies of the Glittering Caves. This is for the scene where they are shepherding the fleeing refugees to safety."

⌂ **THE GLITTERING CAVES**
Digital matte painting
Yanick Dusseault
"This particular one offered quite a
challenge, both technically and
artistically. The camera movement had
to be digitally extended to reveal the
painting filling most of the frame. It was
also difficult to find good photographic
reference material for the subterranean
environment – the result was therefore
entirely handpainted."

**THE GLITTERING
CAVES**
Digital artwork
Alan Lee
"This artwork was used as
the basis for Yanick's final
matte painting [above],
which was later composited
into the shot where the
Rohan civilians seek refuge
during the Helm's Deep
battle."

HELM'S DEEP
Color studies
Jeremy Bennett

"Here we have Aragorn riding over this beautiful environment and we were thinking about dropping Helm's Deep in the background. So I was wondering how far away Helm's Deep was. Was it half a day's ride away? Was it half an hour? This would have ended up as a matte painting, so I was thinking of the overall color palette — three distinctly different feels, all quite subtle. I also had to consider the time of day: we know where the sun is, we know how it will be affecting this rockface — adding this information makes it a lot easier for shooting the miniatures and for everyone else concerned. So doing this kind of painting is a form of problem-solving."

ROHAN PLAINS
Digital composite
Matt Welford (Comp)
& Joosten Kuypers (Massive)
Aragorn sees the approaching massive Uruk-hai army making their way towards Helm's Deep.

URUK-HAI ARMY
Pencil sketches
Warren Mahy
"Man, a huge crossbow!
These two weapons were
designed before I'd read the
script, and before we knew
how much was going into
Helm's Deep. So it was just
a concept that maybe they'd
brought along siege
machines and they might
have been able to see a bit
more of what they were
doing by being behind the
lines rather than at the wall
of Helm's Deep. Basically,
they're just big versions of
crossbows — big double
crossbows that have a lot
more power to them."

URUK-HAI ARMY
Saruman's bomb
Gareth Jensen
"This is the device that Saruman uses to blast
through the wall at Helm's Deep."

URUK-HAI ARMY
Pencil sketches
Warren Mahy
"These are some of the final Uruk-hai drawings I did. I love the concept of the helmet covering the eyes of the Uruk – it's a very scary look. We get toward the final design with the three headshots below, where you can see the development of the crest on the helmet."

URUK-HAI ARMY
Pencil sketches
Ben Wootten

"This was when we were beginning to look at the idea that the Uruk-hai are more organized than the Orcs, and there was going to be a breakdown of the various different troops in the Uruk army, so there's a halberdier and a swordsman. There was also going to be a bowman over on the right. We wanted to feel that there was more of a structure to these guys, they'd been trained to be more ordered, more disciplined."

HELM'S DEEP
Maquettes
Various

Daniel Falconer
(right): **A concept for an Uruk-hai Officer. His fabric bears the brass of his rank.**

John Howe
(facing page – left): **This maquette is very close to the final Uruk-hai design.**

Ben Wootten
(facing page – right): **A design that followed Warren Mahy's drawings. It was affectionately named 'His favourite guts'. This provided a strong look for the Berzerker helmet.**

URUK-HAI ATTACK
Pencil sketches
Warren Mahy

"Once again back to the idea of tribal, with their tops protected more than their legs. I guess for these guys it's for ease of movement, because they've still got to have the strength to carry the armor as well as everything else. The guy below is a Berserker, a type of Uruk-hai trooper that isn't from the books directly. I think Pete wanted the idea that you had these guys that were shock troops, that they were totally expendable. They were bigger, almost like the odd one out of the bunch that was slightly more warped — you know, psychos . . ."

◊ **URUK-HAI ARMY**
Pencil sketch
Daniel Falconer

"This guy was rejected just for having a bit of a Mad Max-y feel, but it was just exploring an alternative idea. He still has the White Hand of Saruman on his belly-plate. This was going with a quite impersonal executioner-style look. He has armor more on one side than the other — heavy drapes of chain and thick leather. I assume that this type of fighter would have a one-sided fighting style where they would advance side-on, all in a row, so the enemy would be presented with quite a small target. Therefore, all his armor is concentrated on his leading edge."

URUK-HAI ARMY ◊
Designs
Ben Wootten

"The Uruk-hai were the first army we designed, the first sets of armor; the brief was to make them look real, not Dungeons and Dragons. At this point we hadn't met John Howe or Alan Lee, and so had very little appreciation for armor; therefore what we thought was looking quite real wasn't! And so we have studs on the leather, and these silly little leather plates. We learned from John particularly — he's a great medieval reenactor and armor expert — he'd come in and say, 'What are you thinking there!?' So it's very funny to look at this. One thing I like — and I still think works quite well — is the color. That rusty brown — it's a nice color for Uruk-hai.

"Even back then, we had that distinct sword — it was on one of Jamie Beswarick's maquettes. I thought it was amazing, because if you were designing a sword for these guys, the cleaver is fantastic — it's just so simple. They are fighting horsemen a lot, so with that spike you could rip someone off a horse, hook them off, and then punch through their armor, because a fine point can punch through armor a lot quicker than a blade. It's a beautifully utilitarian weapon.

"He's got a wooden shield. We know that Saruman tore down a massive amount of trees to fuel the furnaces below Isengard, so there's a lot of timber to hand. It's an available resource, pretty easy to make, so that was it."

URUK-HAI ARMY
Pencil sketches
*Ben Wootten &
Warren Mahy*

"With this sketch on the far left, we were doing sword design, still resolving how much armor they might be wearing on their arms, and the general cut of the helmet. The swordsman has splints down his arm, which is a very simple but quite an efficient way of stopping your arm getting chopped off, and then there's the shape of the breastplate. We were still trying to establish a look for these guys, straight back, very powerful shoulders, as opposed to the slinky Orcs."

URUK-HAI ARMY
Maquette
Jamie Beswarick

URUK-HAI ARMY
Pencil sketch
Ben Wootten

"Ah, the Berserkers. The heavy shock troops wearing masks — there was that very simple clean face with just the little eyeholes and the space for the mouth. And there's something kind of creepy about the simplicity of it. It also ties in with the fact that they're easy to make; Uruk-hai armor can be mass-produced. And it's really impersonal — you get no impression of what's going through the mind of your attacker, which is something you use in combat all the time. The thing I like about the weapon is that, for the Uruk-hai, it's such an intuitive-looking weapon, it doesn't look like it needs any skill to wield it. It's just a huge, heavy piece of steel. You can see you don't need fencing lessons!"

URUK-HAI ARMY
Designs
Daniel Falconer

"Some early designs for Uruk-hai armor: padded, studded, black leather, with some chain — taking the leap from what was initially described in the book, which I think is loads of dark leather and chainmail, and then seeing where we could go with it. I was exploring quite a square cut with these — an officious or military look as we identify it today, with high boots; ultimately, that wasn't the way we went."

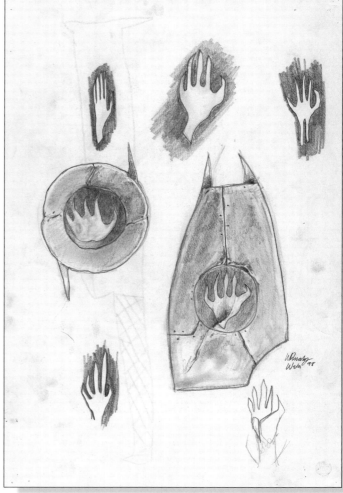

URUK-HAI ARMY
Designs
Warren Mahy

"We were starting to play around with the Hand — the White Hand of Saruman — on them. They were all painted by hand on the props and the actors, so that's why they are all slightly different — we wanted that variation. The Uruk-hai themselves would have painted each other, so different-sized hands would result in different-sized Hands!"

URUK-HAI ARMY
Designs
Daniel Falconer

"A lot of designs were done for the crossbows. This is one of the more industrial looking. Industry was a theme for the Uruk-hai, so we thought that if any of the races of Middle-earth were going to carry a crossbow, it would be the Uruk-hai. We explored just how industrial we could get before they became too modern or too eighteenth- or nineteenth-century."

URUK-HAI ARMY
Color sketch
Daniel Falconer
"If you drop in subtle cues that people identify with already, it can succeed in eliciting certain emotional responses. For example, the high boots on this Uruk are reminiscent of those worn by a German soldier. So, by subtly inserting little cues like this into the armor designs, you can make an audience feel a certain way about a character very, very quickly, and they don't even realize that you're doing it if you're clever enough. That's what we try to do with these characters, but ultimately, in this case, it wasn't really quite the look or feeling that we wanted for the Uruk-hai, so it was abandoned."

HELM'S DEEP
Pencil sketches
Alan Lee

"The two pencil drawings on this page were done during my first week of work on this project. They were still quite exploratory. I felt I knew what the wall would look like, but I'd never done a detailed drawing of the Hornburg. The digital study below is almost a fisheye-lens view of the set in its environment, covering the full extent of one of Peter's crane shots and replacing the containers and catering tents with what we'd like to see in the finished shot."

HELM'S DEEP
Pencil sketch
Alan Lee

"An aerial view of Helm's Deep. We were still refining the details, but we felt close enough to a final design to start visualizing it in color, and this was a preparatory drawing for a watercolor. I added in Gandalf on Gwaihir because we were also looking at those Isengard scenes at the same time and I thought it would be nice to see him flying over the Hornburg."

This idea was not developed.

HELM'S DEEP
Pencil sketch
Alan Lee

"The armory, like much of the interior of Helm's Deep, is carved into the mountainside. This was just the bare bones of the set. We built wooden racks and Weta supplied a massive amount of weaponry and equipment to arm the refugees."

HELM'S DEEP
Color study
Jeremy Bennett
"This is the end frame of a shot that starts at the head of the valley: ten thousand Uruk-hai are marching past, the camera follows them in and reveals Helm's Deep in the distance."

◊ **HELM'S DEEP**
Digital artwork
Gus Hunter
"Peter had found a great location for
Aragorn's arrival at Helm's Deep, and this
was one of a number of studies showing
how the miniature would fit into this
environment."

HELM'S DEEP
Color study
Jeremy Bennett

"The top painting is a reverse of the armies facing each other. At this stage the Uruks are coming out of a layer of mist, so we're just starting to spot them. We're seeing their flames and maybe the front row. At this stage, no one but Aragorn has any idea as to the numbers actually coming, so they're frightened, but still oblivious to the full horror."

HELM'S DEEP
Compositional studies
Jeremy Bennett

"These are two shots that show all the characters — the Elves on the Deeping Wall, the Rohirrim up on Helm's Deep itself, and the Uruk-hai — all facing off to each other. These were done, because the figures will all be CGI, to give the guys in Digital an idea as to where they'll be placed. Pete had specific instructions as to where they were in the shot — just past the Causeway, just before the Causeway, higher up . . . wherever he felt they looked best.

"It's also to give a feeling for the overall palette as well as a sense of atmosphere. The whole environment is actually incredibly dark, and the tricky part — or the challenge — was to really show off the elements we were building or adding.

"These Helm's Deep paintings weren't done as a lighting guide as such — they were more for composition, and to give an impression of what might be visible in the shot."

HELM'S DEEP ◊◊
Pencil sketch
Alan Lee

HELM'S DEEP
Color study
Jeremy Bennett
"This is a color palette for the sequence where Gandalf and the Rohirrim charge down the slope to save the day, because at this stage you have Théoden and the guys doing their final charge into the Uruk-hai. So what we're looking at here is the position and the angle of the Helm's Deep miniature, which will be a guide for Alex Funke to shoot it, and the amount of light that's striking it, so it's lighting stuff for them. It'll be a great shot and great sequence, actually, one of the best."

HELM'S DEEP
Finished digital composite
Alan Lee

HELM'S DEEP CAUSEWAY
Digital artwork
Alan Lee
"These images are a guide for the digital artists compositing the shots in the dawn charge sequence, and for the placement of the massive, the created digital Uruk-hai soldiers."

HELM'S DEEP
Digital artwork/sketch
Alan Lee
"Placing Gandalf and Shadowfax on top of the shale slope, and on the right, following the charge down into the Uruk masses. This was done in order to help Miniatures complete their match-moved shots."

KX.50:2971
20:05:54:2

357.5/4 first frame

KX.50:2971 0513+02   224
20:05:59:03.

357.5/4 mid frame

KX.50:2971 0518+10   224 0566+10
20:06:02:16.   00001120

Helm's Deep Shale Slope charge - sc.357.5/4 ver. 1
Pan from left to right.   AL   17/12/01

HUORNS AT HELM'S DEEP
Color studies
Jeremy Bennett

"This painting above is a quick color study based on one of Alan Lee's drawings, with the emphasis on Helm's Deep at dawn, at the far end of the valley. In the foreground you can see the Uruks retreating into the forest. The trouble is, that forest wasn't there when they arrived . . .

"To the right is another painting looking the other way, which offers a panoramic view of all the Huorns that have filled the valley."

◁◁ **GOLLUM**
Digital composite
Alan Lee
Frodo, Sam and Gollum at
the Black Gates.

GOLLUM ▷
Design sketch
Jamie Beswarick
A very early design sketch.

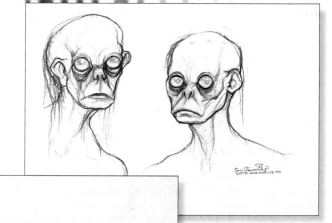

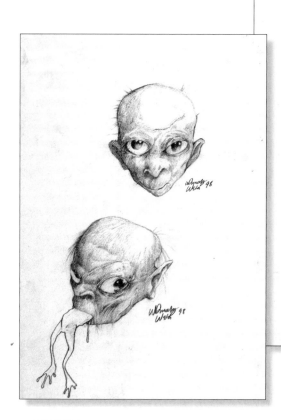

◇ **GOLLUM**
Pencil sketch
Christian Rivers

◠ **GOLLUM**
Design sketches
Warren Mahy
"The thing that I always fought with Gollum was the fact that he had
such big eyes and a little nose; to most people that means 'cute.' I
was trying to get that craftiness and that smartness in there, and the
fact that he could strangle anybody if he got his hands on them!
I think I was giving a bit of age to him as well. He has a less skeletal
look than a lot of other people have done."

   (Center right) "I was just trying to bring a bit of the character up.
The conflict between Sméagol and Gollum — you can imagine the
frustration that he would feel at those times where he 'crosses
over' and Sméagol remembers Gollum and Gollum remembers

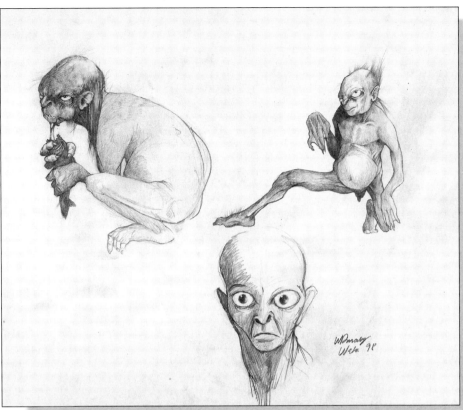

GOLLUM
Design sketches
Warren Mahy

"These were done at the same time as the Gollum eating the frog" (facing page). "Again, it's that childlike face, before it became emaciated.

"The picture below was done quickly – basically just a costume design. A couple of ideas for the loincloth. I liked the idea of it being a shirt and still having pockets and varying degrees of wear and tear."

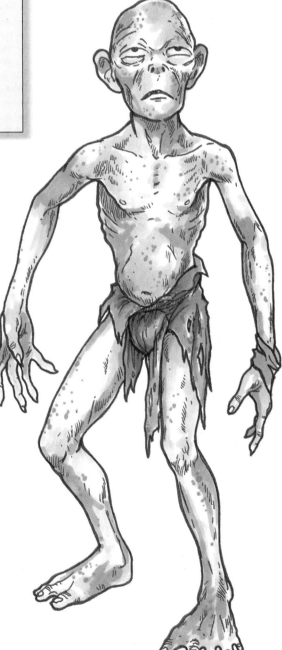

△ GOLLUM
Pencil sketch
Daniel Falconer

"It became very apparent early on that Jamie Beswarick and Mike Asquith were capturing Gollum quite well with the designs they were doing. This was one of my early versions – too thin and ill-looking."

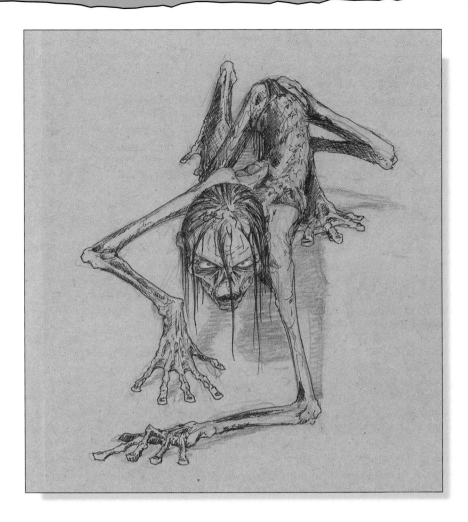

GOLLUM
Design sketches
Daniel Falconer

"Gollum was always one of my favorite characters when I read the books, but as it was, I actually didn't do a great deal on him. In retrospect I think some of my concepts were a little off target – perhaps a little bit too emaciated. In particular these ones looked less like a hobbit that has turned into something, and more like some kind of new creature entirely. Up until this point, nobody had started looking at the color scheme on Gollum, so I thought I would. In this particular case, the idea was that his skin, while once flesh-toned, has now changed. He's been out in the wilds a long time, so it's almost like grass stains have worn into him from running around in the dirt, and there's very little of the actual flesh tone left. Again, this probably has the effect of making him a little bit too 'monstery.' The final design we went with did actually have a very pale flesh tone, rather than the green."

◊ **GOLLUM**
Design sketch
Ben Wootten

"I like this one of him on the tree branch. You can imagine him sneaking around Elven forests, just spying on people. He looks also a lot healthier in this picture. I imagine that it is probably earlier on in Gollum's story, where he's still in reasonably fertile lands, and there's plenty of bird nests around, plenty of young rabbits, so he's probably quite well fed. Later, of course, when he hasn't eaten for days, and he won't eat the Elven food, he's quite drawn. That's a very strong feeling I took from the book – that toward the end it's sheer force of will that's keeping him alive. Clinically, he's probably dead!"

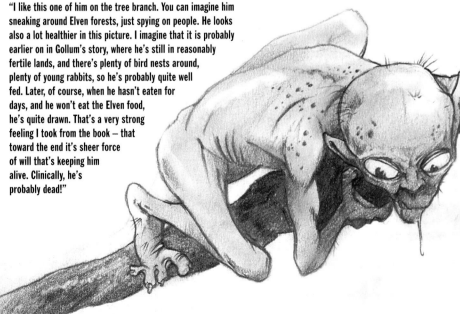

GOLLUM
Design sketch
Warren Mahy

"I think the fantastic thing about this project has been the fact that we have had so much time to develop characters, and the philosophy seemed to be – with the design – not to spend too much time putting gloss into the illustration but to have the shapes right, the shape of the face or size of the body."

GOLLUM
Design sketch
Ben Wootten

"The idea of designing Gollum was a massive challenge but I enjoyed taking it on. Because everyone has thought about him, everyone has a preconceived idea, so actually realizing the guy is incredibly difficult. And I think in that respect we were all keen to have a go and get our ideas out there, because obviously we all had differing views on what he looked like. The other thing that is cool about him is that he's probably the most tragic character in all the books. Tolkien doesn't write people's thoughts in his books, it's old saga style, but you get inside Gollum's head because he's schizophrenic, he talks to himself. He's the only character where you see his thought processes working; I think that draws you to him as well."

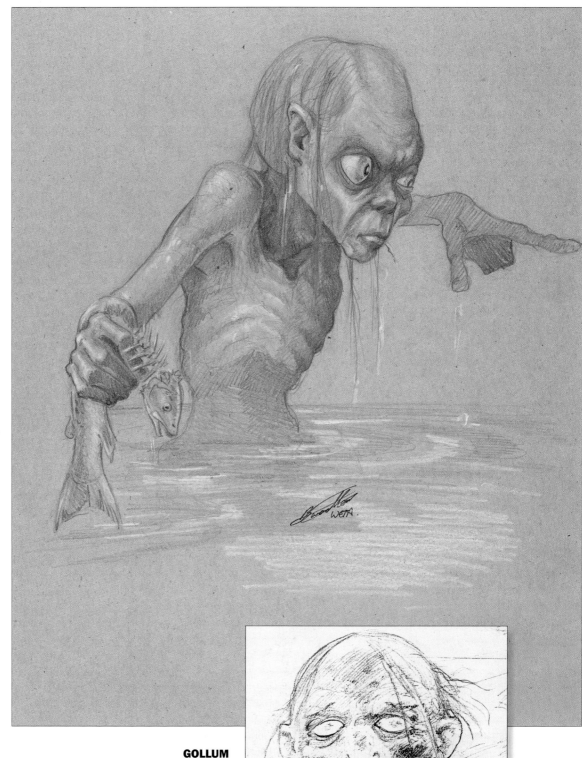

GOLLUM
Pencil sketch
John Howe

"At one point, it seemed like everyone was doing Gollums. Poor Gollum was one of the hardest creatures to pin down, thin, wiry and slippery as he was."

GOLLUM
Pencil sketch
Daniel Falconer

"It was decided that the skeletal nose here was a little bit too zombielike. We determined early on that it was probably necessary to give him a human nose; otherwise he becomes too unsympathetic. Also, he's got that bloated potbellied look, something that was introduced in a design that Warren did, which we pursued for a short while. And with this particular character, there is almost the idea that he'd have a tiny little gut, because obviously he doesn't eat very much, but when he does eat it all swells up — but the idea didn't get very far."

⬆ **GOLLUM**
Pencil sketch
Ben Wootten

"This is an early look at him — it epitomizes Gollum, big toes, big spindly fingers, big eyes. As with an earlier sketch of mine, I imagined him as malnourished — too thin perhaps, but still dangerous."

◁ **GOLLUM**
Design sketches
Warren Mahy

"Just very quick Gollums to show facial expressions — neither of which were very relevant, but they were still fun to draw!"

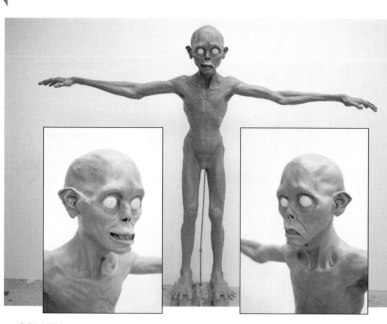

GOLLUM
Pencil sketch
Alan Lee

"This drawing above right was done while Jamie Beswarick was working on his full-size scannable maquette (above). The sculpture has quite a presence. It is the size Gollum would be if we were hobbits."

To the right is a selection of Film 1 and Film 2 Gollum body proportion comparisons by Weta Digital.

GOLLUM ▭
Digital animation puppet
Bay Raitt & Jason Schleifer

Below is an example of the interactive "ridged" puppet used by the animators at Weta Digital to animate Gollum in Film 1.

GOLLUM
Expression studies
Mike Asquith
"Once the first incarnation of Gollum was decided upon, Pete wanted to see him pulling various expressions. I was given photos of Pete making all the expressions he wanted to see. From those photos I produced these six plasticine sculptures."

☖ GOLLUM
Pencil sketches
Alan Lee
"These character studies were done while we were thinking about changing Gollum's design for <u>The Two Towers</u> so that he would more closely resemble Andy Serkis."

GOLLUM
Sculptures
Bill Hunt (top right) &
Jamie Beswarick (middle)
Two versions of the early Gollum in expressive mode.

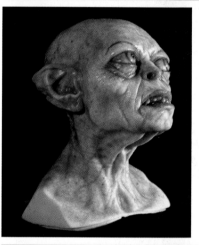

▽ GOLLUM
Sculptures
Jamie Beswarick
Below are some examples of the reworked maquette, which more closely resembled actor Andy Serkis.

GOLLUM ◊
Silicon head
Jamie Beswarick & Gino Acevedo
Final head design (right and opposite) – designed and sculpted by Jamie Beswarick and painted by Gino Acevedo: "After designing several different paint schemes for Gollum, this is the final 'look' that Peter approved."

GOLLUM
Still frame from
The Two Towers
Weta Digital

GOLLUM

Various artists

"It became apparent as the character of Gollum developed, that the original creature, barely glimpsed in <u>The Fellowship of the Ring</u>, would need to be changed. Although everyone loved the first Gollum, he was created before Andy Serkis arrived on the scene and astonished us all with the emotional strength of his performance.

"We knew that a lot more work needed to be done on the textures and finer details but Christian Rivers suggested a more fundamental design change that would enable the puppet to match the range of expressions and the subtlety that Andy bought to the role.

"Bay Raitt, who modelled and set up Gollum's CG face, worked closely with Peter and Fran Walsh, as well as with Jamie Beswarick and Christian, on the finer nuances of Gollum's characterization.

"Simultaneous to this effort, the articulation of Gollum's body was built by Jason Schleifer and Paul Story and the Creatures department under Eric Saindon using the muscle and skin system developed by Richard Addison-Wood.

"The new Gollum was brought several steps closer to reality through the process of texture painting and shading by the 'look' department, under the guidance of Gino Acevedo and Joe Letteri.

"Once the Digital puppet was complete, the animators led by Randy Cook, brough the performance to screen either through keyframe animation, motion capture or by rotoscoping the exact movements that Andy made on set. Randy Cook and the animation department had a monumental task in bringing to life a character who has so much emotional and physical contact with his fellow co-stars.

"Bringing all of these elements together is another huge job in itself and the hard work done by the compositors, lighters, rotoscopers, paint artists, matchmovers, and the dozens of hard working individuals involved in every aspect of the process has helped to set a new benchmark for film-makers to aim at.

"When the Cabbalist, Rabbi Loew of Prague fashioned his Golem out of clay, the final spell that brought it to life was written on a piece of paper, and placed under its tongue. For us, that final spell is the script, and the story, and what makes all our efforts worthwhile is knowing that we were working on, and part of, a good story, well told."

Alan Lee

GOLLUM
When things went
wrong
Bay Raitt
"A collection of humorous digital mishaps."

GOLLUM
Digital shader tests
Steve Demers
& Ken McGaugh
"Gollum's eyes and teeth took the award for the most remodeling and tweaking."

GOLLUM
Digital designs
Bay Raitt
"These two images [above and opposite bottom] show the differences between the film 1 and film 2 Gollum. The most significant changes were smaller eyes, wider cheeks and a larger forehead plane."

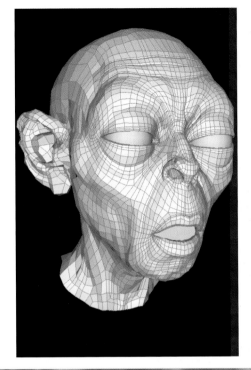

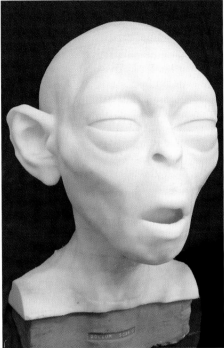

GOLLUM
Digital sculpting meets physical sculpting
Bay Raitt & Jamie Beswarick

"Once we were happy with the way the digital model moved (above left), a relaxed expression was output in physical form by using a laser-gel printer (center).This model was then cast in clay and detailed using traditional sculpting tools (right). The result was then scanned back into the computer and applied to the animated digital model to create final surface contours seen in the movie."

GOLLUM ▷▷
Built from a cube
Bay Raitt

"These snapshots illustrate the building of Gollum's digital face from a cube primitive using Mirai. On the facing page are photos of final design maquettes by Jamie Beswarick of the approved film 2 sculpt taken to aid Bay Raitt's initial digital Gollum."

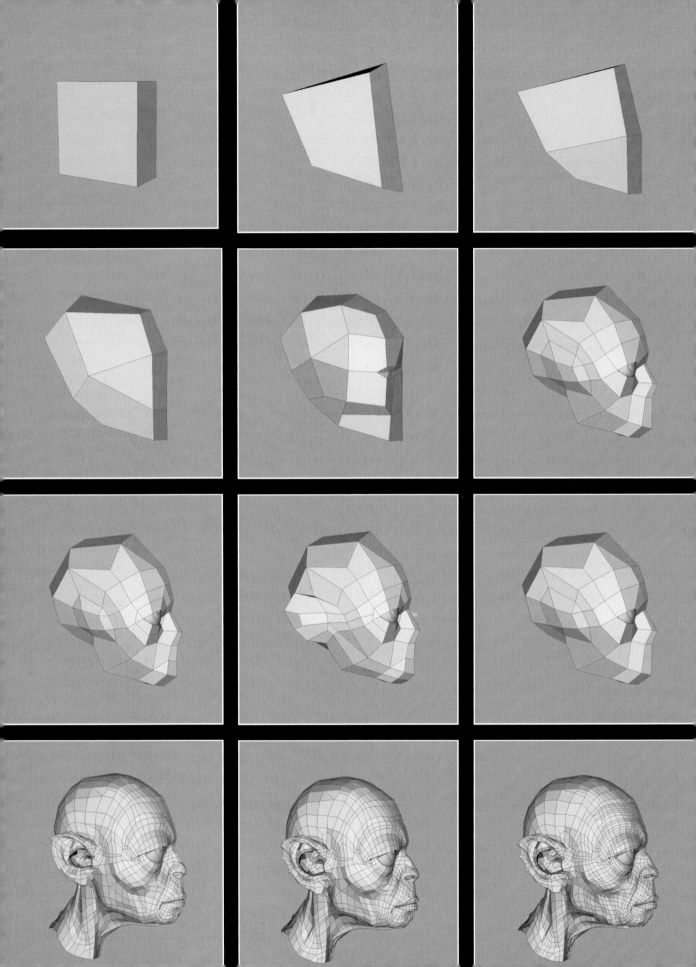

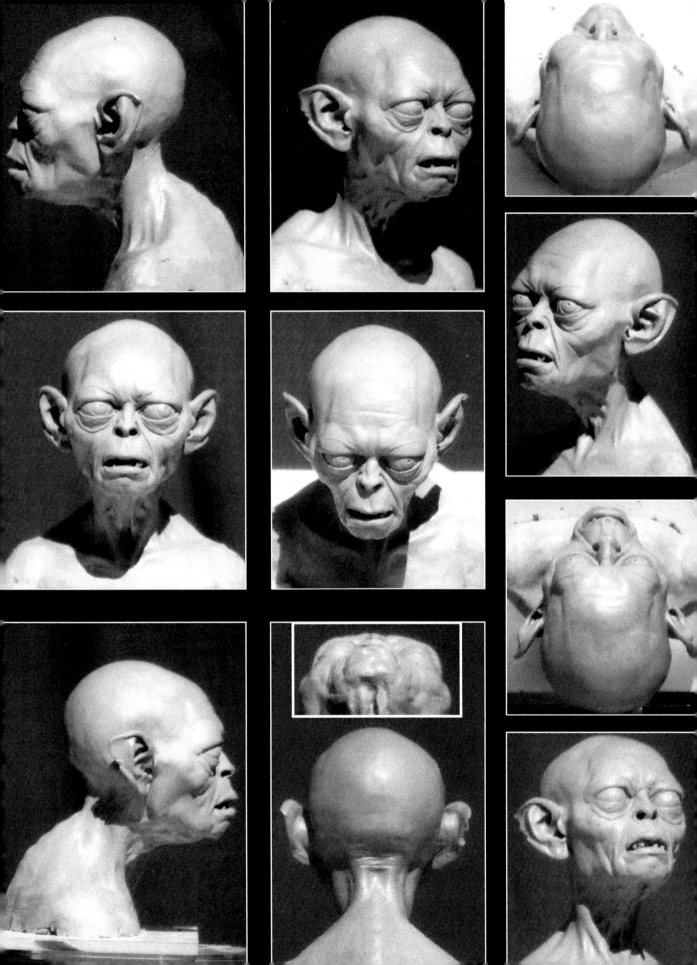

Afterword

The long quest for the quintessential Gollum was already well under way by the time I arrived in New Zealand to begin principal photography. I wasn't exactly sure what he was going to look like (and little did I know that I would be joining a process that would take a further two and a half years to finally bring the tortured creature to life). However, within hours of getting off the plane, I found myself sitting in a preview theater with Richard Taylor and Director of Animation Randy Cook. They showed me a fully animated test shot of Gollum: "This is where we've got to at the moment, but there's gonna be some changes – we're not sure about the size of the pupils." My eyes opened wider than even Gollum's could – I had never seen anything like it in my life, and any misgivings I'd had previously about the poor soul being computer-generated immediately vanished.

Even from a cursory reading of the books, Tolkien's love of the character is obvious. He gives us his idiosyncratic speech and countless descriptions of his physicality, making him so memorable. He loyally invests him with such wretched pathology, pain and pathos. These were obviously first base as a way into playing the character, but for me one of the most important keys to how I thought Gollum would actually move and sound came from the artists' sketches, and from one pencil drawing in particular.

We see him, broken, head lolling to one side, mouth open as if wailing in pain, like a recently liberated victim of torture, or a homeless heroin addict, the weight of his racked mind and body almost pinning him to the rocks he sits on.

It haunted me, and drove me to the conclusion that we should always see the creature on all fours. The physical wear and tear on his body, combined with the pain of rejection, withdrawal from the loss of the thing he loved and hated and his self-loathing at what he had become, had reduced him to a crawling thing, never standing on two feet as he did before he became corrupted by the Ring. It was a major character decision, inspired by one of the films' conceptual artists, John Howe.

My collaboration with the films' artists and animators grew when we worked on the descent of Sméagol into the madness of Gollum (including a whole team of prosthetic artists, with genius Gino Acevedo at the helm). Then Christian Rivers, Richard and Peter had the idea to make Gollum's facial structure closer to mine, so that he could be made to take on my expressions. Enter animator Bay Raitt, whose job it was to study my every lip curl and cheek raise and translate them to controllable faders on the computer for the creature's makeover. Randy and I had already formed a very close relationship early on – he was my touchstone and fellow Gollumite – and between us we would try to scratch our way under the little fella's skin.

After Peter had decided that he wanted to use motion capture on a greater scale, my circle of workmates increased, with a studio full of amazing digital artists and technicians (Moggey, Frank, Ivan, Remington – you rock!). In order to take Gollum to this next level, environments spatially identical to the original sets I'd acted on with Elijah and Sean maybe a year previously were constructed. I would then act the scenes again, on my own, in their entirety, wearing a suit fitted with light-reflecting sensors. Every movement I made was picked up through the twenty or so cameras and relayed into computers, which in turn fed the information to the CG Gollum puppet on screen. In real time. I became a kind of actor/puppeteer at this stage. The motion was then captured, processed and edited. And then after that, with an ever-growing shanty town of animators drafted in to work on Gollum, we all batted off each other, trying to really make each second on screen as truthfully animated, captured and acted as possible. We would talk one-on-one and collectively, examining every dramatic beat and moment of every scene, in the context of the arc of Gollum's journey, giving the character depth and learning how to let the subtext play – either using the essence of how I had performed it on set as a basis or else directly matching it frame for frame. Then, of course, the components had to be assembled, and so over it went to Randy, Joe, Jim and their team. It was the most curious but amazing marriage of skills, and incredible for me as an actor to follow the creation of my character from a pencil sketch to a fully functioning digital creation that was every bit as real as the actors it was playing opposite.

Working with these artists has been quite awe-inspiring – every single time you'd walk through the doors of Weta and Weta Digital, you'd get a massive buzz from the people, their passion and their art. It really does blow you away. It's such a melting pot. Only here could you meet so many experts, be they leaders in their craft or blazing young talents, under one roof – and I feel deeply privileged to have been so closely associated with them.

Talk to almost anyone who worked on these films and they will tell you that the traditional, limiting barriers of "job description" seem to have fallen away, allowing artists and technicians (and, in my case, an actor) to cross over into areas of creativity not normally associated with their own field of expertise. This in turn allowed imaginations to flourish and knowledge and craft to be exchanged at the same time. Everyone has had the ability to be not too – well, precious, if you'll pardon the pun, to commit totally to vast amounts of work, knowing that perhaps only the tip of the iceberg of their endeavors will ever be seen.

These films, and the artwork that surrounds them, are a celebration of process. Not settling for the first idea, but expanding the imagination, sharing one's passion with trust, finding a shared truth. This book is a wonderful opportunity to marvel at the rich bedrock of material created by the awesome talents of Christian Rivers, Jeremy Bennett, Mary Maclachlan, Ben Wootten, Warren Mahy, Yanick Dusseault, Paul Lasaine,

and of course the wondrous John Howe and Alan Lee (to name but a few). Every single sketch, storyboard, maquette and miniature has worked its way into a collective consciousness that created the movie's Middle-earth, and therefore is absolutely a part of its fabric. And yet they all stand up as works of art in their own right, and you'd kill to have any one of them up on a wall in your home!

In times as dark as these that we live in, where the prism through which we see the world has narrowed into good/evil, black/white, we have no forum for coming together to find new ways of thinking. Because of this, cinemas, theaters and galleries have become more and more important as places for learning about and understanding our humanity. World leaders and politicians keep falling into the old traps time after time, leaving it to artists, musicians, filmmakers and writers to help us through – those who choose the world of the imagination, rather than a knee-jerk response to that which surrounds us. The *Lord of the Rings* experience is all about the fueling of that imagination.

Three years ago, a film director who was interviewing me for a role in his new movie said to me, "Artists are terrorists . . . the truth is our bomb." (He was going to make a highly politically sensitive movie in an incredibly dangerous part of the world, and he had extremely partisan views.) My immediate thought was, "This man has a death wish and doesn't care who goes down with him." I did admire his determination, but not his politics. I left the interview and, not surprisingly, never heard from him again. A few weeks later I was sitting in a room with Peter Jackson and Fran Walsh talking about *The Lord of the Rings* and Gollum. Their passion and profound understanding of the world they were about to bring to the screen overwhelmed me. I also felt that I had met two incredibly special people. And fortunately they gave me the opportunity to become part of a great artistic endeavor, where I could meet and work with immensely creative people, artists who are not terrorists but seers, whose truths are not bombs but gates opening up a pathway to the imagination.

Andy Serkis
London, 2002

Credits

THE LORD OF THE RINGS
THE TWO TOWERS

Conceptual Designers
Alan Lee
John Howe

Production Designer
Grant Major

Costume Designer
Ngila Dickson

Visual Effects
Jim Rygiel

Director of Miniatures Photography
Alex Funke

WETA WORKSHOP LTD

Special Make-up, Creatures, Armor, Weapons and Miniatures Effects Supervisor
Richard Taylor

Designers/Sculptors
Mike Asquith
Jamie Beswarick
Shaun Bolton
Daniel Falconer
Warren Mahy
Ben Wootten
Sacha Lees
Johnny Brough
Sourisak Chanpaseuth
Bill Hunt
Ben Stenbeck
Christian Rivers

Senior Prosthetics Supervisor
Gino Acevedo

Senior Miniature Technicians
Mary Maclachlan
Paul Van Ommen
John Baster

THREE FOOT SIX LTD ART DEPARTMENT

Props Designers
Gareth Jensen
Adam Ellis

VISUAL EFFECTS ART DEPARTMENT

Visual Effects Art Directors
Jeremy Bennett
Paul Lasaine

Photoshop Artist
Gus Hunter

Visual Effects Consultant
Mark A. Stetson

WETA DIGITAL LTD

Supervising Storyboard Artist
Christian Rivers

Visual Effects Supervisor
Joe Letteri

Visual Creature Effects Art Director
Gino Acevedo

Animation Design & Supervisor
Randall William Cook

Creature Supervisor
Eric Saindon

2D Supervisor
John Nugent

Motion Capture Supervisor
Remington Scott

3D Sequence Lead TDs
Ken McGaugh
Guy Williams

3D Lead TDs
Steve Demers

2D Sequence Leads
Colin Alway
Mark Lewis
Charlie Tait

Creature Facial Lead
Bay Raitt

Head of Matte Painting
Max Dennison

Senior Matte Painters
Yanick Dusseault
Roger Kupelian

Matte Painters
Deak Farrand
Mathieu Raynault
Laurent Ben-Mimoun

Massive
Joosten Kuypers

Senior Compositors
Jon Bowen
Matt Welford

To be continued in . . .

THE LORD OF THE RINGS

The Art of
THE RETURN OF THE KING

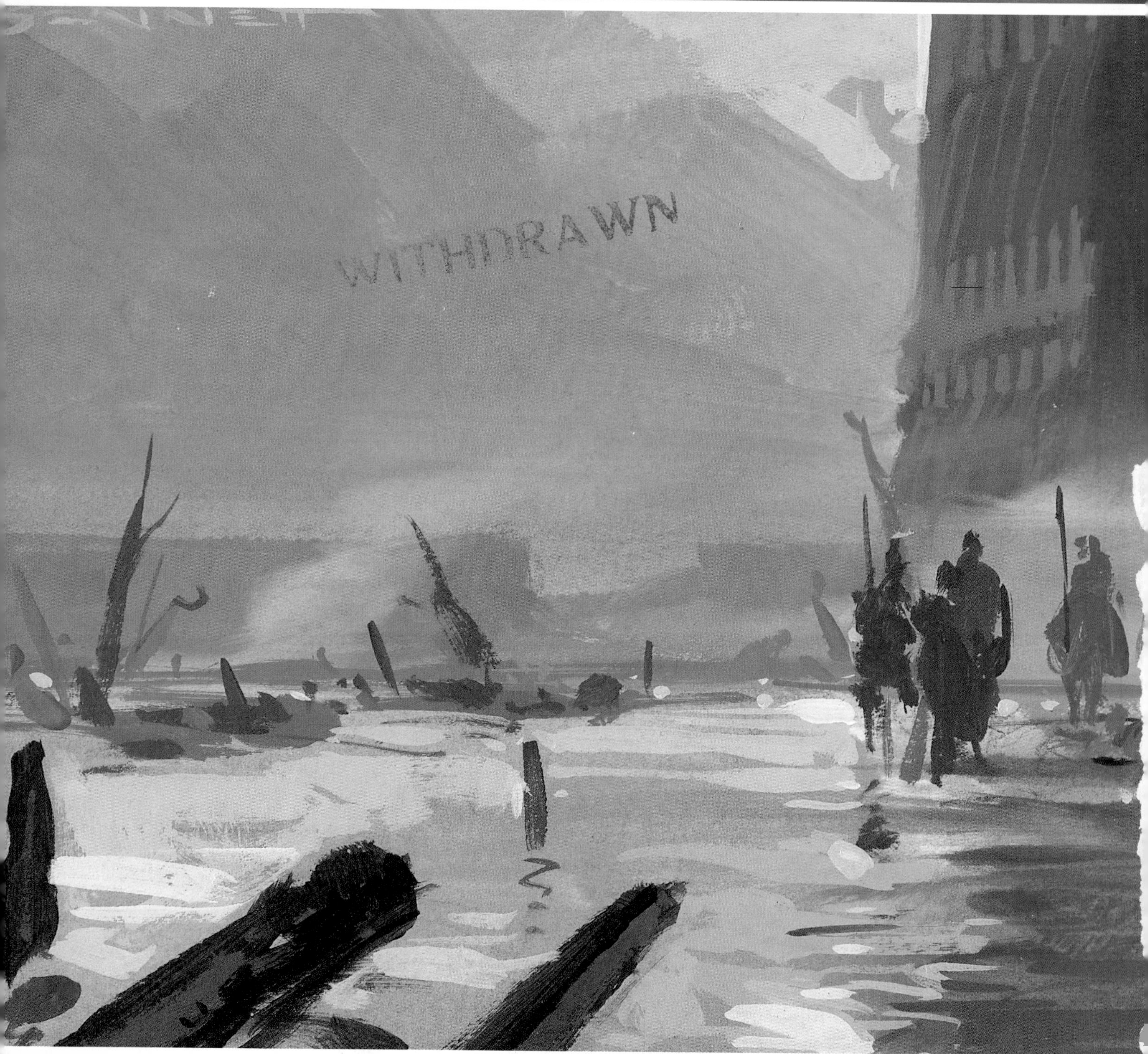